A COLLECTION OF
THANKSGIVING
Blessings

Inspiration and Encouragement
for a Season of Gratitude

BARBOUR
PUBLISHING

Our mission is to publish and distribute inspirational products offering exceptional value and biblical encouragement to the masses.

Printed in the United States of America.

The Power of
THANKSGIVING

INTRODUCTION

Every year we celebrate in abundance—turkey and all the trimmings, decadent slices of pumpkin pie, time spent with family and friends, fellowship, football, and thanks to the One who provides it all.

From the breath in our lungs to the beauty of the sunset, we have much to be thankful for. Honoring God with thanksgiving is something that takes more time and effort than one prayer at one meal, one day a year. Thanksgiving is a powerful act of sacrificial worship that should be a part of our daily lives. Scripture says that God's will is for us to give thanks in every situation (1 Thessalonians 5:18). The Bible also tells us that offering thanks to God truly honors Him (Psalm 50:23).

He's worthy of all the thanks we can offer.

"But giving thanks is a sacrifice that truly honors me.
If you keep to my path, I will reveal to you
the salvation of God."
PSALM 50:23 NLT

Thankful for All

*Thou preparest a table before me in the presence of
mine enemies: thou anointest my head with oil;
my cup runneth over.*

PSALM 23:5

Some people never find satisfaction in the things they do have, but spend their entire lives wishing for things they don't have. They are never happy with where their lives are going; they feel empty in their relationships, and therefore they find it impossible to give thanks for the many blessings they have been given.

As Christians, we are to be people of praise. Every prayer we offer unto God should acknowledge the many wonderful things that He has done for us. Not even a blind person can deny the beauty and splendor of this world. God gives good things to His children, and we should be thankful for all that we have.

*Lord, I cannot believe how much I have been given. Help open my
eyes to the many blessings that have been bestowed upon me. Make me
thankful, Lord. Amen.*

Satisfaction Guaranteed

Oh, satisfy us early with Your mercy,
That we may rejoice and be glad all our days!
PSALM 90:14 NKJV

You've probably bought items that guaranteed you'd be satisfied. If you weren't, the manufacturer promised, you could get your money back. But how many people bought an item, weren't satisfied, and found the company didn't live up to that promise? We've often found, to our discouragement, that people aren't what they seem and disappear as soon as they've cashed the check or processed the credit card information.

But God isn't like that. He's always what He says He is, and He's gone to great lengths to tell us about Himself. He even sent His Son to clearly show us what He's like. Jesus died for us to give a clear picture of how much He wanted to share our love.

Earthly guarantees often don't give us satisfaction, but when we read His Word and get to know His Son, we quickly comprehend the difference between people's promises and God's. Even when the rest of the world disappoints us, we can cling to Jesus and be glad to the very end.

Have you experienced God's mercy and accepted His love? Then your satisfaction is guaranteed. He promises you'll never be left or forsaken (Hebrews 13:5). Joy in Him will be your portion for the rest of your life.

Impossible Tasks

So the wall was completed on the twenty-fifth of Elul, in fifty-two days. When all our enemies heard about this, all the surrounding nations were afraid and lost their self-confidence, because they realized that this work had been done with the help of our God.
NEHEMIAH 6:15–16 NIV

Under Nehemiah's leadership, the people of Judah had rebuilt Jerusalem's wall in fifty-two days. Facing opposition had only spurred them on. Though half the workers had to stand by fully armed to fend off attack, they'd accomplished their mission. In record time, the wall was standing.

The nations around Judah didn't like it one bit. But it wasn't because of something powerful about the people of Judah—no, they feared this nation because it was clear God had helped them.

Do you face an impossible task today? Perhaps you need to get some work done before the end of the day, and you don't see how you'll do it. Start by asking for God's help, then work as hard as you can, giving your best. But when it's all done, don't expect that you have no more to do. Give God the praise in a tactful way. Perhaps you only need to say, "That was an answer to prayer," but somehow let the message that God was with you be known.

Thank You, Lord, for helping me with impossible tasks.
To You, nothing is impossible.

Reasons to Give Thanks

FOOD ON OUR TABLE
*And having food and raiment
let us be therewith content.*
1 TIMOTHY 6:8

GOD-GIVEN TALENTS
*But now hath God set the members every one
of them in the body, as it hath pleased him.*
1 CORINTHIANS 12:18

A PLACE TO WORSHIP GOD
*I was glad when they said unto me,
Let us go into the house of the LORD.*
PSALM 122:1

God's Handiwork

And the heavens shall praise thy wonders, O LORD:
thy faithfulness also in the congregation of the saints.
PSALM 89:5

The rainstorm had been terrific. Torrents of rain had fallen, drenching everything. Now the clouds began to part. Shafts of bright sunlight stretched to the earth, causing all foliage to sparkle with droplets of water. On the horizon, a rainbow stretched from earth to earth. The clouds climbed high into the sky, turning rosy pink with the sunlight.

God's creation gives testimony to His truth all the time. All His wonders unfold through the course of one day. From the sunrise through nighttime starshine, God's glories unfold. Take time to view God's handiwork. Search the daytime skies and see the majesty of the Almighty. His hand is ever upon His creation.

All praise and honor belong to You, Lord, for the magnificent works of your hands. You have made such beauty, and You have loved us enough to share it. Thank You, Father. Amen.

He Is Worthy

Offer unto God thanksgiving;
and pay thy vows unto the most High.

PSALM 50:14

Early Christians suffered terrible persecution, even death, for refusing to bow down to idols. Images of Caesar were prominent throughout the Roman Empire, and all were expected to pay tribute to these graven images. The Christians refused, and so they were thrown into jail, and sometimes they were thrown to wild beasts. God was so important to these early Christians that they could not offer tribute to anyone less worthy.

Only God is worthy to be praised. In all we do and all we are, our lives should pay tribute to God. Nothing else is good enough. Offer to God thanksgiving and praise, for He alone is deserving.

Thank you for the gifts You give, Almighty God. From the rising of the sun to its setting in the night, I will praise You for all that You have done. Glory is Yours, Father.
Amen.

Real Thankfulness

Behold, he smote the rock, that the waters gushed out, and the streams overflowed; can he give bread also? Can he provide flesh for his people?
PSALM 78:20

Brittany wanted a car, and she got a car. She wanted to go to an expensive college. She wanted her own apartment, and Daddy came through with the money. She wanted nice clothes, a stereo, a cell phone, a microwave, a television. There was no end to Brittany's wants. Nothing satisfied her. No matter how much she was given, she wanted more.

We need to be careful that we don't approach God that way. God wants us to truly appreciate what we have before we start asking for more. He gives good things to His children, and He is willing to give abundantly, but He desires us to learn the real meaning of thankfulness.

Dear God, make me appreciative of all the wonderful gifts You give. When I take things for granted, show me the error of my ways. Fill my mind and heart with gratitude for the many blessings I have. Amen.

Blessed

Honour and majesty are before him:
strength and beauty are in his sanctuary.
PSALM 96:6

Take time to be quiet and think about the good things God has done for you. Look at both the good times and the bad times in proper perspective. We are loved by a God of all creation, the Master of all eternity. He has made us important by His love for us. Think of how wonderful this love is. We have no way to comprehend this kind of love and attention. It was good to take time to contemplate all these things. All honor and glory belong to the Lord, who loves us so much. By entering into His presence, we come to know just how very blessed we are.

Who am I, Lord, that You take notice of me? I cannot believe that You love me the way You do. Though I don't understand, I do accept Your gracious love, and I am thankful from the depths of my soul. Amen.

Prayers of Thanks

Your Word is my daily nourishment, Lord. Thank You for the Bread of Life that You provide every single day. Those words feed and nurture my soul just as eating bread fills me and provides the nutrition I need to live. Without Your words I will fade and die spiritually; with them I am vibrant, energized, and alive! Be my portion, Lord, as I seek You. And not just Your hands and what You give, but also Your face, Lord. I desire to know who You really are.

> *Jesus answered, "It is written: 'Man does not live on bread alone, but on every word that comes from the mouth of God.'"*
> MATTHEW 4:4 NIV

Lord, I thank You for my salvation. I thank You for Your indescribable gift of eternal life and the power to do Your will today. I can hardly fathom how you suffered, yet you did it all for me—for every person on this planet. Mocked and beaten, You bled for my sins. You had victory over death so I could live. You made a way for me, and I am eternally grateful. Thank You, Lord.

> *Thanks be to God for his indescribable gift!*
> 2 CORINTHIANS 9:15 NIV

Make a Difference

Blessed is he that considereth the poor:
the LORD will deliver him in time of trouble.
PSALM 41:1

Curse the beggars! It was impossible to go anywhere without seeing someone with his hand out. Ted refused to look into their faces. He despised people who were always looking for a handout. He worked hard for what he got; why couldn't they? It made him so mad. He rounded the corner and abruptly stopped in front of a young boy who was obviously very ill. The boy looked up into Ted's face and sobbed one word: "Please?"

All the excuses, all the anger, all the contempt melted away. Ted's eyes were opened for the first time. These people really needed help, and he had the power to make a difference. Perhaps he couldn't solve the whole problem, or even a big part, but he could help the boy and his mother. With new resolve, Ted swore to open his eyes to the less fortunate and give as much as he could.

Father, am I doing all I can? In my times of need,
I cry out for someone to help me. Make me
sensitive to others as they cry out. Amen.

Bountiful Harvest

The pastures are clothed with flocks; the valleys also are covered over with corn; they shout for joy, they also sing.
PSALM 65:13

Each year the rice paddies were laid out and the tender plants were planted. Each year the people of the village waited with anxious hope, looking to see whether the storms would come and wash the fields away. Many times the people would watch as their hard labor was destroyed, but other times they rejoiced to see their crops full and bountiful. After each harvest, the village offered a portion of its harvest to God, thanking Him for His mercy and grace.

What do we offer to God when we are blessed with good things? Do we even remember to say thank you? The Lord has given us so much, and we should always and everywhere give Him thanks and praise.

In bad times, please be my strength; in good times, celebrate with me, Lord. Thanks for being with me, doing so much for me, and giving so much to me. Amen.

Daily Purpose

This is the day which the LORD hath made;
we will rejoice and be glad in it.
PSALM 118:24

Rainy days are loved by farmers. Snowy days are loved by children who can stay home from school. Storms are loved by mystery fanatics. Gray days are loved by romantics. Sunny days are loved by picnickers. Warm days are loved by beachgoers. Cool days are loved by those who stroll. All days have their purposes under heaven. Enjoy the day that the Lord has made. He has many more to share.

Let me appreciate the gift of this day, Lord.
Help me to use my time wisely, teach me to rejoice,
and fill me with joy that never ends. Amen.

Beyond Our Asking

More than hearts can imagine or minds comprehend,
God's bountiful gifts are ours without end.
We ask for a cupful when the vast sea is ours
We pick a small rosebud from a garden of flowers,
We reach for a sunbeam but the sun still abides,
We draw one short breath but there's air on all sides
Whatever we ask for falls short of God's giving,
For His greatness exceeds every facet of living
And always God's ready and eager and willing
To pour out His mercy, completely fulfilling
All of man's needs for peace, joy, and rest,
For God gives His children whatever is best.
Just give Him a chance to open His treasures,
And He'll fill your life with unfathomable pleasures—
Pleasures that never grow worn out and faded
And leave us depleted, disillusioned and jaded
For God has a storehouse just filled to the brim
With all that man needs, if we'll only ask Him.

HELEN STEINER RICE

Daily Bread

Blessed be the Lord, who daily loadeth us with benefits,
even the God of our salvation.
PSALM 68:19

When we ask God for our daily bread, what do we mean? Is it merely food to nourish our bodies? Is it all the basic necessities of life? Does it include the bread Jesus spoke of: the Word of God? It is all these things and more. Our heavenly Father wants us to have everything we need to affirm His image within us. God never calls His children to tasks they are not ready for, and He will not abandon us without the resources we need to succeed. Our God provides us with everything we need to be the best people we can be. Call upon the Lord to load you daily with benefits. He will do even more than you expect.

Lord, I do not even know what I need to be better
than I am today, but in Your wisdom, You see my every need. Give me
what You will, in order that I might honor and glorify You. Amen.

Beautiful Truth

How sweet are thy words unto my taste! yea,
sweeter than honey to my mouth!
PSALM 119:103

The singer spun a tale of joy and triumph. The audience sat enthralled by the young woman's voice. She painted a picture lovelier than words. The senses came alive as she performed her art. The sights, sounds, colors, smells, and tastes burst forth through her song. She sang from her heart, and her story was shared by many. Emotions connected, and the entire crowd—singer and audience—moved together in a spiritual harmony. The experience was electrifying.

When we are in the presence of truth and beauty, it is undeniable. A chord is struck within us all. That chord is the image of God in each of us. We connect with the universal rhythm that God set in time long, long ago. The result is joy—a sensation and a feeling that defies explanation—but assures us of the reality of God. Open yourself to His truth.

There are times when I feel Your presence so strongly, Lord. I know
that You have orchestrated a masterpiece of which I am a small but
important part. Thank You for including me. Amen.

Immediate Blessings

However, as it is written, "No eye has seen, no ear has heard, no mind
has conceived what God has prepared for those who love him."
1 CORINTHIANS 2:9 NIV

God has future blessings in mind for you, but did you realize that this verse is also talking about things you can experience today? Read the context of this passage, and you'll notice that Paul isn't talking about the sweet by-and-by—he's describing his current ministry and the work of the Spirit in the lives of Christians.

If you've been waiting for heaven to enjoy all the joys and delights of faith, look around. Note the blessings you've received today, all the things God has done and is doing in your life, and appreciate them. But don't stop there; you can also start taking advantage of the spiritual mission God has given you. Because God never gives us blessings simply to enjoy—every good thing is meant to be shared.

You don't have to look to another Christian to discover what God has for you. No one in this world can tell you what He has in mind. Verse 10 says God reveals these unseen gifts by His Spirit.

Go to the real source—God. If you ask, He'll show you the gifts He's given and how He wants you to influence others with them.

He has wonderful things in mind for you, so don't wait until eternity—share some of that good news today!

Always Blessed

In the day of prosperity be joyful, but in the day of adversity consider:
Surely God has appointed the one as well as the other, so that man can
find out nothing that will come after him.
ECCLESIASTES 7:14 NKJV

Sometimes our souls don't feel particularly satisfied. It's hard to feel very peaceful when we lose a job, wonder how we'll pay the rent, and imagine all kind of dire results. Prosperous days seem to lie behind us, and we can't look into the future and tell how long we'll be in this situation.

God doesn't allow us to look into the future. That's a good thing, because if we knew the future, we wouldn't need to trust God. One of His best methods of developing our spiritual lives would no longer exist, and we'd enter heaven as weak, spineless beings—not the strong ones He wants us to become.

But whether our present is joyful or sad, God still remains faithful. He provides for our needs even if we don't get the lavish things we'd prefer. And He always provides generous spiritual blessings for those who trust in Him. Like Paul, who experienced prosperity and want, we can do all things, when we abound in Christ (Philippians 4:12–13).

No matter what your circumstances, you can always cling to Jesus—and be blessed.

Reasons to Give Thanks

TIME SPENT CONVERSING WITH GOD
*I love them that love me: and those
that seek me early shall find me.*
PROVERBS 8:17

LETTERS FROM A LOVED ONE
*Heaviness in the heart of man maketh it stoop:
but a good word maketh it glad.*
PROVERBS 12:25

INSPIRING, CARING TEACHERS
*Give instruction to a wise man, and he will
be yet wiser: teach a just man, and he
will increase in learning.*
PROVERBS 9:9

Accepted by God

"I was sought by those who did not ask for Me;
I was found by those who did not seek Me. I said,
'Here I am, here I am,' to a nation that was
not called by My name."
ISAIAH 65:1 NKJV

None of us was really searching for God when He found us. Though we may have begun to feel empty inside, we didn't know where to go. Then God brought along someone who told us that He loved us and wanted to share our lives with us. We heard the good news that He wanted to heal and forgive us.

We don't come to God with any status. Everyone comes as a poor, empty sinner. Out of that, God builds a new life. Do we show that truth in our living? Can we accept others, no matter how rich or poor they are, no matter what background they come from? Or are we haughtier than God, requiring financial "perfection" or a certain "acceptable" background of our friends, fellow church members, and acquaintances?

God sought us—unloved, unappealing, seemingly valueless sinners—and gave us all His love. He saw something in us when no one else could. Can't we do the same for all those who touch our lives?

Thank You, Lord, for accepting me just as I am.
Let me live humbly in Your spirit, with love for all.

God's Help

"First here, then there—you flit from one ally to another asking for help. But your new friends in Egypt will let you down, just as Assyria did before."
JEREMIAH 2:36 NLT

When trouble comes, to whom do you go? Jeremiah saw God's people running all over the ancient Near East, looking for help from various powerful nations. As an unstable political situation threatened Judah, it searched for security—in all the wrong places. As Jeremiah prophesied, the nation was eventually led into exile, because instead of looking to God, it looked to other people (2:37).

Getting some support from others is a good thing. We all need help at home, on the job, and in the community. And offering help to others is the right thing to do. But there are things no human can help us with—solutions no person can come up with. Ultimately, if we trust our lives to anyone but God, we're looking for safety in the wrong place.

No matter what challenges you face today, have you asked God for help? Whether it's tutoring one of the kids in math or painting the house, have you placed your day in His hands?

If so, you need never despair: He will help you today.

Thank You, Lord, for always being willing to come to my aid. Help me accomplish all I really need to do today.

Strength

A gracious woman retaineth honour:
and strong men retain riches.
PROVERBS 11:16

Judas Iscariot possessed qualities that Jesus considered worthy, or he never would have been selected as a disciple. Judas followed faithfully for the better part of three years as he shared in the ministry of Christ. At a time when he should have been strongest, he proved weak. He gave in to the temptation of the sparkle of silver, and he betrayed his friend and Lord. He had lived so very close to the true treasure—the love of Jesus Christ—and he threw it all away due to his weakness.

Everyone sins. That is sad but true. Often we are weak when we want to be strong. It is vital that we hold on to the love of God in those times when we are most sorely tempted. God offers us His strength when our own strength is not enough. When we call on God to help us in our weakness, then we have found true wisdom and strength. If we will deal honestly with God, He will shower us with treasure that cannot be taken from us and honor that testifies to the glory of Christ.

O Lord, I pray that I might make You proud of me.
I will try to please You by my actions and praise You with my words.
Be with me, Father. Amen.

Prayers of Thanks

Lord, what a blessing that You have given us such an array of emotions with which to express ourselves. Help me to be more like You—slow to anger and abounding in love. Help me to be forgiving. I pray for more discernment, so that in whatever comes my way I will have the grace to think, speak, and act with a good and godly attitude.

> *"The LORD is slow to anger, abounding in*
> *love and forgiving sin and rebellion."*
> NUMBERS 14:18 NIV

Lord, I thank You for my home. Show my heart opportunities to open this home to others. I want to share what You've provided for me. As I practice hospitality, may Your love shine through my life. However my home compares to others', I thank You for what I have. I am grateful that Your Spirit is present here. Give me a generous, open heart, and use my home for Your good purposes.

> *Share with God's people who are in need.*
> *Practice hospitality.*
> ROMANS 12:13 NIV

Ours for a While

The earth is the LORD's and the fulness therof;
the world, and they that dwell therein.
PSALM 24:1

Two families disputed for years about who held claim upon a
stretch of fertile land. Harsh words and insults were exchanged
regularly, and on occasion, tempers flared to the point of physical
violence. Neither family would budge in their conviction that they
were the rightful owners. No compromise could be reached, and so
the seeds of bitterness took root between the two clans.

Long after the two families are but faint memories, the land
will still be there. How foolish it is to devote so much of our lives
to the acquisition of things, when it all truly belongs to the Lord.
We are but caretakers of what the Lord has made, and it has been
given to us for everyone's pleasure. Wise use of our resources and
preservation of all creation is the responsibility of all humankind.
We have been given many precious gifts, but they are ours for only
a while. In time, all things return to the Lord.

Lord, make me a wise steward of Your creation.
Let my actions hurt not one living thing.
Help me to build up, rather than destroy.
Inspire me to share, to give, and to love. Amen.

A Faithful Blessing

And he blessed Abram, saying, "Blessed be Abram by
God Most High, Creator of heaven and earth."
GENESIS 14:19 NIV

Read through the story of Abraham and his family, and you'll find repeatedly the words *bless, blessed,* or *blessing.* God made it abundantly clear He wanted to do wonderful things for these people.

Yet sometimes being blessed by God still has its difficult moments. Abraham and Sarah received a promise—a child would be theirs, despite the fact that both were elderly. But time went on, and the promise wasn't fulfilled. Like most of us, this couple didn't want to wait. So they decided to take control of the situation, and Sarah gave her maid, Hagar, to Abraham. However, the child the maid bore was not the babe of promise, but a terrible problem for the little family and the nation it became. It's to Ishmael, Hagar's son, that the Arab nations trace their heritage.

God's blessing doesn't mean we can't make mistakes and pay a price for them. Like Abraham, we can get ourselves in awful trouble. But we can be sure God will be faithful with His blessing. "The LORD had blessed [Abraham] in every way," records the scripture toward the end of Abraham's life (Genesis 24:1). Despite the mistakes, God still loved him and gave him great blessings.

God has blessed us with a relationship with Him. He is faithful to us, too. Let us walk faithfully in His way through all our days.

All Good

Everything God created is good, and nothing is to be rejected
if it is received with thanksgiving.
1 TIMOTHY 4:4 NIV

Has God given you good things? In our culture, that often implies a huge house, a fancy car, and steak for dinner. But haven't you had a house you loved, even though it wasn't in the finest part of town, an older car you didn't want to get rid of, or a macaroni-and-cheese dinner that fed your stomach and your taste buds as well as any steak? Good things don't have to cost a lot of money.

Your best relationships are priceless. Would you trade a much-loved parent for money or a spouse for gold? These, too, are gifts from the heavenly Father, who knows how to give the best—no matter the cost.

And what of the other things God creates that have no price? A sunset filled with vibrant colors, a drink of water that quenches thirst as no man-made beverage can. God has given generously in many more ways than we often consider.

But no matter what God gives us, we are to receive it with thanks. He made it just for us, and we're enjoying the benefit, so why not share that joy with Jesus? He's the best gift God had to offer—and the only gift we truly need.

Nice Deal

The LORD also will be a refuge for the oppressed,
a refuge in times of trouble.
PSALM 9:9

Ellen lived in a tiny shack on the edge of a small backwater town. She had no modern conveniences, no car, no electricity, no fancy clothing. She just lived a simple life, sharing what little she did have with anyone who needed it. Often people tried to help Ellen, but she just smiled and said she didn't need anything. When asked why she lived as she did, Ellen said, "God has made sure that I've had enough to get by on. I don't need any more than that. He and I have a nice deal. When He needs me, He lets me know and shows me what I can do; and when I need Him, all I have to do is call. I've faced hard times, but the Lord has always given me strength and given me a place to run to."

The Lord is our refuge and our strength. It takes a great deal of wisdom to realize that. Our lives are much more than possessions and positions. We need not ask what more God can do for us, but what we might do for God.

Father, I sometimes need to escape: from the world,
from myself, from the things that tie me down.
Be my liberation and my sanctuary. Strengthen
me for Your service. Amen.

Reasons to Give Thanks

TIME SPENT WITH FAMILY

Blessed is everyone that feareth the LORD;
that walketh in his ways. . . . Thy wife shall be as a fruitful vine
by the sides of thine house: thy children like
olive plants round about thy table.
PSALM 128:1, 3

A GODLY MENTOR

Where no counsel is, the people fall: but in
the multitude of counsellors there is safety.
PROVERBS 11:14

PRODUCTIVE GARDENS

Build ye houses, and dwell in them;
and plant gardens, and eat the fruit of them.
JEREMIAH 29:5

Funny Creatures

Whatsoever the LORD pleased, that did he in heaven,
and in earth, in the seas, and all deep places.
PSALM 135:6

Imagine the fun the Lord had creating all the animals of this world. With the power to do whatever He pleased, He concocted a menagerie of some wonderful creatures. Consider the giraffe, or the baboon, or the frog. What a host of funny-looking creatures. Think of the splendor of the eagle, the grace of the gazelle, the power of the tiger. God put so much into making His creation a good one. The same is true of His children. God went to great lengths to make sure His children were good. He even imparted to each and every one of them His own image. He offered them free will and all the blessings they could ever hope for. He did these things because they pleased Him. Our God is a God of love, and nothing pleases Him more than to be able to share that love. Indeed, we may be God's funniest creatures, but that only makes Him love us all the more.

Father, You must have a wonderful sense of humor to put up with
children like me. Forgive me for being less than You created me to be.
Help me to grow and mature and develop into Your image. Amen.

Best Love

Because your love is better than life,
my lips will glorify you.
PSALM 63:3 NIV

Nothing in this world is better than knowing God.
Perhaps, with all the delights of this world, that sounds a little strong. You may be in no rush to enter heaven and lose the things you've worked hard for and the earthly blessings God has given you. But if you can remember back to the days before you knew God, think of the difference He has made. Would you go back to life before Jesus?

Once Jesus enters a heart, losing life becomes but a painful moment that opens the door to eternity. Eternal delights for the Christian cannot compare to anything here on earth—even the best of the blessings God has already given us. Our hearts are no longer earthbound, and we long to be with him. When He calls, we cannot imagine staying in this world without His blessing.

Though we may not rush to leave the fellowship of friends and family, the beauty of the world, and so much more that God has given, like the psalmist, we appreciate that anything that lacks Jesus is less than the best. Life here, without God's love, would be meaningless.

David had his priorities straight when he wrote this. Even being king of Israel, with all its benefits, wasn't better than loving God. So during his life, he praised his Maker. And in eternity, he's praising still.

Basic Needs

O God, thou art my God; early will I seek thee: my soul
thirsteth for thee, my flesh longeth for thee in a dry
and thirsty land, where no water is.
PSALM 63:1

The rock face extended straight up. Terry was halfway up, and his arms ached. From the ground it hadn't looked nearly so high. The sun was scorching, and all Terry could think of was a cool drink of water. He would give anything to be able to stop and drink, but there was no safe place to do it. The more he thought of water, the worse his thirst got. He comforted himself by thinking the next drink he took would be the best he'd ever had.

We often don't appreciate the simple things in life until we are unable to enjoy them. Clean air, water to drink, food on the table; these things come easily to most of us, and so we are not as thankful as we might be if we didn't have them. Many in our world have to do without. Remember that even the most basic of our needs is met by the loving grace of God. Thank Him for everything He has given you.

For the air that I breathe, the warmth of the springtime sun,
the food that nourishes me, and for so much more, I lift my
voice in thanks and praise to You, Lord. Amen.

Prayers of Thanks

Lord, I thank You for my good health. It is a blessing. I pray for Your power to sustain me as I take care of myself—by eating healthy food, drinking enough water, and making movement and exercise a part of my daily life. Give me the self-control and motivation I need to make wise choices to support the health of my mind, my spirit, and my body. Please keep me from injury and illness, and keep me safe, I pray.

Say to him: "Long life to you! Good health to you and your household! And good health to all that is yours!"
1 Samuel 25:6 NIV

Lord, I thank You for giving me hope. I don't know where I would be without You. I don't know what the future holds, but You give me the ability to be joyful even while I wait—even when I don't understand. Please help me to have a positive attitude and live with a mind-set of patience and courage as You work Your will in my life. Help me to remain faithful in prayer, Lord, and fully committed to You.

Be joyful in hope, patient in affliction, faithful in prayer.
Romans 12:12 NIV

Joy and Love

O come, let us sing unto the LORD:
let us make a joyful noise to the rock of our salvation.
PSALM 95:1

The children lined up on the steps to the altar. Their freshly scrubbed faces shone in the morning light. Nervously, they swayed, twitched, and squirmed. The music began, and each child in turn joined in at a point of his or her own choosing. Some sang out boldly, others mouthed the words, while a few ignored the songs altogether and just waved and smiled at Mommy and Daddy. To call the presentation "music" was stretching the point, but to call it a joyful noise was right on target. The spirit of the children was joy and love, and the hearts of all present were captured quickly. The sound rose to the rafters and beyond. The Lord heard that special choir, smiled, and said, "It is good!"

Let the words of my mouth produce a joyful noise,
acceptable to the Lord and glorifying to
Him in all ways. Amen.

Beautiful Conclusion

*Now to him who is able to do immeasurably more
than all we ask or imagine, according to his power
that is at work within us, to him be glory in the
church and in Christ Jesus throughout all generations,
for ever and ever! Amen.*
EPHESIANS 3:20–21 NIV

Have you ever had God answer a prayer you hadn't even gotten around to praying yet? Maybe the problem was on your mind. You mulled it over, but somehow it never made it to your prayers, perhaps because the world got in the way. By the time you got to formal prayer, it had slipped off into mental oblivion.

Then one day you learned that God had been at work all along and solved the problem you had shelved. The situation came to a beautiful conclusion without your having prayed at all. How awful you felt that you had never even brought it before the Savior!

None of us should ignore prayer, and it's a good idea to keep a prayer list at hand; but even when we fail, God doesn't. We may ponder something without prayer, yet in His grace He answers even that unspoken need. He does immeasurably more than we think to ask for. How much He deserves our praise!

*I praise You, Lord, for doing more than I'd even
think of asking for. I give You all the glory.*

Pleasing to Him

Blessed is every one that feareth the LORD;
that walketh in his ways. For thou shalt eat
the labour of thine hands: happy shalt thou be,
and it shall be well with thee.
PSALM 128:1–2

Jack sat down to supper with his family. Even after twenty years, there was something special about a meal that came from their own farm. Jack could imagine thousands of families sitting down to similar meals of produce from his farm. It made him feel like there was purpose to his life. The work was hard, and there were worries about the future, but it was all worth it. The farm was Jack's life.

Many people find no satisfaction in the work they do. Their lives lack purpose and meaning. But Christians have an alternative source of meaning in their lives. If a Christian does a job—no matter how large or small—to God's glory, that person will find satisfaction. If we do our work without grumbling and with a joyful heart, we are witnesses to His power in our lives, and we are pleasing to Him.

Do not let me be so concerned with the prestige of my job,
or the salary it pays, or what other people think of it. Instead, assist me
to always do the best that I can, to Your glory, Father. Amen.

He Never Gives Up

Nevertheless my lovingkindness will I not utterly take from him, nor suffer my faithfulness to fail.
PSALM 89:33

Amy tried everything she could to get the little boy to learn to tie his shoes. She had sat with him for hours. There was nothing she could do to make him understand. Finally, she lost all patience and walked off angrily. His shoe-tying education would have to come from someone else with a lot more patience and endurance!

We may give up on each other, but it is comforting to know that God never gives up on us. His offer of forgiveness is open to us today and every day to come. Even though we reject the offer or do things that are frustrating and displeasing to Him, He never gives up. He asks us daily to follow Him until the day we finally do. Thank goodness His patience is without bounds.

Though I push the patience of others to the limits, I am glad to know that I have not pushed Yours, Lord. Continue to forgive me, Lord. I am weak and foolish, and only Your great love keeps me going. Amen.

Reasons to Give Thanks

GOD'S PROMISES
The Lord is not slack concerning his promise, as some men count slackness; but is longsuffering to us-ward.
2 PETER 3:9

THE DIVERSITY OF THE FOUR SEASONS
Thou hast set all the borders of the earth:
thou hast made summer and winter.
PSALM 74:17

A VOICE TO SING SONGS
I will be glad and rejoice in thee: I will
sing praise to thy name, O thou most high.
PSALM 9:2

God's Triumphs

Not unto us, O LORD, not unto us, but unto thy name give glory,
for thy mercy, and for thy truth's sake.
PSALM 115:1

Max had worked at the mission for over forty years. There had been weeks on end when he hadn't even gotten to go home. He lived to serve the poor and homeless in his area. When he finally decided to retire, the entire city pitched in to pay him tribute. Throughout the proceedings, Max seemed uncomfortable, and finally he stood to speak.

"I don't want to seem ungrateful, but all this really isn't necessary; and besides, I don't really deserve it. God is the One who needs to be honored. I have just been fortunate enough that He has used me all these years. I really haven't done anything special; I just did what God wanted me to do."

It is difficult to set aside our own egos in order to serve God freely. When all is said and done, however, all that we are able to do is made possible by God's grace. Our triumphs are God's triumphs. Like Max, we should feel privileged that God has chosen to work with us and through us.

Use me, Lord. With the gifts and talents You
bestowed upon me, enable me to spread Your
good news to everyone I meet. Amen.

A Perfect Gift

*The LORD is my strength and my shield; my heart
trusts in him, and I am helped. My heart leaps for
joy and I will give thanks to him in song.*
PSALM 28:7 NIV

Have you ever felt as if you should give thanks but your heart just wasn't in it? Perhaps at Christmastime you received a gift that was somehow less than perfect.

Giving thanks on such an occasion becomes difficult. The giver may suspect you aren't thrilled with the gift. But you still try to express the appreciation you *do* feel.

God never gives us the wrong gift. He never wraps up another item of clothing to fill our already overstuffed drawers. Instead, He recognizes the intangibles we never have enough of and presents them at the moment of need. When we lack strength or protection, He is there for us.

A much needed gift received at the perfect moment is always welcome, even if it comes at no special holiday. God knows that—and understands the importance of timing for everything He gives. His presents are always timely, always perfect, and are certain to be received with thanks by a heart that is truly His.

Your heart jumps with joy at His presents, doesn't it? Then, whether you sing His praises or just pray them quietly, make sure to thank Him for each gift.

Beyond Our Comprehension

Great is our Lord, and of great power:
his understanding is infinite.
PSALM 147:5

The snow was falling in clumps. The blizzard had begun six hours ago, and the world had ground to a halt, at least, the world in northeast New York State. It was astonishing to watch the snow accumulate: not into mounds, but into mountains. Somewhere, Stuart had learned in his childhood that no two snowflakes were ever the same. Incredible! The Lord never ceased to create. Billions of snowflakes fell to earth, and not one matched any other. How could people doubt that some creative force was behind the universe?

When we stop to admire the many miracles in nature, we are met with the indisputable evidence of a mastermind who brought everything into being. The power of the Lord is beyond our comprehension, and His wisdom and understanding are beyond our knowing. We should be thankful that the Lord has given us so much beauty. We are blessed by the Lord's continuing creativity.

Dear Father, you have shared so many good things
with me. Let me fully appreciate them all. Show me
the wonders of this world, and let me receive them with the
wonder and amazement of a child. Amen.

Prayers of Thanks

Lord, I thank You for the joy of answered prayer! You are amazing. I delight in You and thank You with a full heart. I asked and You answered. I receive what You give with a grateful heart. Lord, You are good. You are faithful. You are my joy and my delight. I praise Your holy name. Thank You for filling my heart with gladness, Lord.

> *"Until now you have not asked for anything*
> *in my name. Ask and you will receive,*
> *and your joy will be complete."*
> JOHN 16:24 NIV

Lord, I thank You for the work of Your hands. A wildflower, a mountain scene, the ocean waves on a white sandy beach—the beauty of the earth reveals Your glory. Thank You for the smile of a child, the touch of my beloved's hand, the warmth of our home. I am grateful for the love of friends and meaningful work. You have done great things for us, and we are filled with joy. Thank You for Your many blessings.

> *The LORD has done great things for us,*
> *and we are filled with joy.*
> PSALM 126:3 NIV

Why Give Thanks?

Give thanks to the LORD, for he is good;
his love endures forever.
1 CHRONICLES 16:34 NIV

It's not hard to accept that even something God says *once* in scripture is meaningful. But what does it mean when He tells us the same thing over and over? The words of this verse appear dozens of times.

Think God's trying to get something critical through to us?

Though God tells us repeatedly that He is good and His love never ends, it's strange, isn't it, that every time a war starts, we start questioning that first assertion. Is God really good if bad things happen? Has His love changed? If life isn't going our way, we easily ignore the culpability of humans and throw the blame right on God.

Maybe God repeated this scripture so often because He knows how badly we need it. Satan has such an easy time tricking us that we need to keep reality directly in front of us. So over and over, God reminds us of His true nature.

This is a good verse to memorize, because when Satan starts attacking, we can ask ourselves, *Why should we give thanks to the Lord?* And we'll have the answer, *For He is good and His love endures forever.*

Good Thoughts

Oh that men would praise the LORD for his goodness,
and for his wonderful works to the children of men!
PSALM 107:21

Jay was one of the most unpopular men in the office. He never had a good word to say to anyone. He was critical, snide, self-centered, and jealous. People simply got tired of hearing all the negative comments coming from his mouth. Just once they wanted to hear something good come from his lips.

Negative people get on our nerves quickly. They get on God's nerves, too. He calls us to praise Him and lift our voices in positive ways. If only more people would praise the Lord for His goodness, what a wonderful place our world would become. We need to occupy our thoughts with what is good and turn away from what is bad. Praise God throughout the day and see what wonderful feelings you find along the way.

Erase from my vocabulary all negative words and
from my mind all negative thoughts, Lord. Create
in me a fountain of positive feeling and goodwill.
Share your grace through my witness. Amen.

With Every Breath

Let every thing that hath breath praise the LORD.
Praise ye the LORD.
PSALM 150:6

God looked down upon His creation and saw that it was good. In time, God's creation looked back and saw that God was good. Together they formed a unity of love and devotion. Through their covenant, all creation was brought into harmony. The Lord loves His children, and many of His children love Him back. Praise the Lord with all of your being. With each breath you take, remember that the Lord is God. Nothing you do is done apart from Him. Wherever you go, God is there. He will never leave those who love Him. He gives us new years and new challenges, and He helps us to grow and learn. We can enter new phases of life confident that God goes forth with us. Praise the Lord, one and all. The Lord has been very good to His children.

I thank you for the challenges and joys of yesterday and today. Now I look forward to the future, asking Your blessing upon it. Be with me, Lord, and with all my loved ones. Keep me in your care. Shine Your light upon my path, and make me acceptable in Your sight. Amen.

Choose Happiness

A merry heart maketh a cheerful countenance.
PROVERBS 15:13

You never get mad. You always seem to be happy and having a good time. I don't understand it. I wish I could be like you." The two walked along the beach together.

"It's really not that hard. You just have to decide that you're going to be happy, then do it. I got tired of being unhappy about everything, so I decided to quit," the other answered.

We can decide to be happy. It takes work, but it is a conscious effort that anyone can make. God is the giver of the greatest joy a person can ever know. When we make Him the Lord of our life, He can work within us to fill us with this unspeakable joy. The Lord dwells in joy, and He is well at home in a heart that is happy. When we are truly filled with joy, the whole world can see it. They will notice that we are not like everyone else, and there is no more powerful testimony to the power of God than a smile that cannot be taken away.

Fill my heart with Your joy, O Lord. Change the
light of my countenance to happiness so that everyone will know the
effect You have had on my life. I praise You for Your gracious gift.
Amen.

A Thankful Heart

Take nothing for granted, for whenever you do,
The joy of enjoying is lessened for you.
For we rob our own lives much more than we know
When we fail to respond or in any way show
Our thanks for the blessings that daily are ours—
The warmth of the sun, the fragrance of flowers,
The beauty of twilight, the freshness of dawn,
The coolness of dew on a green velvet lawn,
The kind little deeds so thoughtfully done,
The favors of friends and the love that someone
Unselfishly gives us in a myriad of ways,
Expecting no payment and no words of praise.
Oh, great is our loss when we no longer find
A thankful response to things of this kind.
For the joy of enjoying and the fullness of living
Are found in the heart that is filled
with thanksgiving.

HELEN STEINER RICE

Closer Than a Brother

A friend loveth at all times, and a
brother is born for adversity.
PROVERBS 17:17

He couldn't believe it. He had worked for the same company for almost thirty years, and suddenly they pulled the rug out from under him. He had been a good employee, and he had never made trouble. Now he felt ashamed for no good reason. He didn't know what he would do.

When he saw his brother at his door later that day, tears came to his eyes. Whenever anything had ever gone wrong, his older brother had been there to make him feel better. No matter what happened, he knew he could always count on his brother. He had yet to face any bad situation without his brother to support him, and as long as he could lean on him, he knew everything would be fine.

As children of God, we can be thankful that we have Christ to call a brother. He will be with us in every situation. He will be our support and our counselor. He will listen without judging and will never leave us. He is as true as any brother could be, and we can count on Him to be there for us no matter what.

Thank You for being there when I need You.
You are my strength and my shield.
I am so grateful for Your love. Amen.

Totally Blessed

*Dear friend, I pray that you may enjoy good
health and that all may go well with you,
even as your soul is getting along well.*
3 JOHN 2 NIV

When the apostle John wrote his friend Gaius, he not only wished spiritual blessings on him, but he prayed for his health and that his life would go well, too.

It's easy for us to become so spiritually minded that we forget people's other needs. Because we know faith is the most important thing, we pray for a friend's spiritual condition, but do we also pray that physical needs would be met? Do we ask God to help the new widow financially and emotionally, as well as spiritually? Or do we see that as the responsibility of others? Even if we know she doesn't know Jesus, do we reach out in concrete love that can touch her life in other ways?

God's blessings begin with the spiritual, but they don't end there. We've often had reason to praise Him because He has provided for our physical needs time and time again.

Just as God recognizes the needs of this world, we should, too. We can't separate the body from the soul, and often it's the body's needs that make people aware of a spiritual emptiness. God deals with every phase of our lives, and as we offer Jesus to others, we can do that, too.

Then they can learn what it means to be totally blessed.

The Real Treasure

Keep thy heart with all diligence;
for out of it are the issues of life.
PROVERBS 4:23

Jesus said, "Where your treasure is, there will your heart be also" (Matthew 6:21). Moral poverty occurs when we place things above relationships. Christ sent His disciples out into the world without possessions, but no one in history has known more wealth than those chosen men who walked with Jesus. It is when we walk with Jesus that we discover what true riches are.

It is easy to get distracted by so many things. The "good life" requires money, good looks, nice clothes, the right car, the right house, and the right mate. At least that's what we're led to believe. But it is only when we can free ourselves from the pursuit of such things that we can begin to enjoy life the way God intended it. Money cannot buy happiness, nor can it bring us life. Christ brings us life, and He brings it most abundantly. He is the real treasure, and as long as our hearts remain with Him, our lives will truly be rich.

Dear Father, forgive me when I lose sight of what is really important in life. Help me to keep my eyes focused on Your truth. Enable me to show others that You are the real treasure in life. Amen.

Reasons to Give Thanks

SUNSHINE AFTER STORMS
The day is thine, the night also is thine:
thou hast prepared the light and the sun.
PSALM 74:16

THE ABILITY TO LEARN
A wise man will hear, and will increase learning;
and a man of understanding shall attain unto wise counsels.
PROVERBS 1:5

KIND WORDS
A man hath joy by the answer of his mouth:
and a word spoken in due season, how good is it!
PROVERBS 15:23

Wise Counsel

I lead in the way of righteousness. . .that I may
cause those that love me to inherit substance.
PROVERBS 8:20–21

A poor woman called her children to her soon before her death. She sat them down and told them, "I never had money or nice things, and I'm sorry that I don't have good things to leave you, but I always tried to do what was right by you. If I brought you up right, so that you do what you know is right to do, then I have left you more than any amount of money."

The woman was right. The things money buys are temporal; they wear out, break down, and then they're gone. A good sense of values is worth more than all the money in the world. The greatest gift we can hope to give another human being is that of wise counsel. We often hope that we can leave a legacy—a testament to our life—after we die. We can make our lives an example of the truth of Christ, letting others see just how much Christ can change lives for the better. That is the real treasure, and God gives it freely to all who will take it.

I try to turn my eyes from material gain to true gain: the gain of
eternal life. Help me to follow Your instructions, that I might have
Your righteousness. Grant me a small portion of Your holy inheritance.
Amen.

True Joy

There is that scattereth, and yet increaseth;
and there is that withholdeth more than is meet,
but it tendeth to poverty.
PROVERBS 11:24

During the Great Depression, two families shared a house in Pennsylvania. One family occupied the upper floor, and the other family lived in the lower. The family that lived downstairs was always inviting people in to share what they had. No matter how much they gave, they always seemed to have enough. The family on the upper floor, however, scoffed at the way the downstairs family lived. They stored all extras in a locker in the pantry and gave nothing away. It was not until they found that rats had gotten into their pantry that they were sorrowful for what they had done.

Selfishness leads to despair. True joy comes to us, not from what we own, but from what we are able to give to others. When we give what we have, God will bless us with more, and the blessings will be doubled because of the joy that giving brings.

Take what I have, Lord, and use it for Your glory.
I have nothing except what You have given me.
Help me to share from my abundance, and to give
all that I can to those who are in need. Amen.

Good Things

I know that nothing is better for them than to rejoice, and to do good in their lives, and also that every man should eat and drink and enjoy the good of all his labor—it is the gift of God.
ECCLESIASTES 3:12–13 NKJV

When God gives you a good thing—a new house, a child, or a special job—do you hesitate to enjoy it? Do you feel guilty because you have something another person doesn't have?

Where does the idea that Christians should not enjoy life come from? Not from the Bible. Scripture often speaks of the blessings God gives His people—and some are physical.

That doesn't mean enjoyment is our primary goal in life. We shouldn't mainly seek out wealth and fortune. God describes these things as fleeting, and putting our trust in them will only lead to sorrow.

But that also doesn't mean we shouldn't rejoice when God gives us worldly goods or that we shouldn't make wise use of them. When we thank God for His blessings and use them properly—to help others and support our families in a responsible Christian lifestyle—those temporary things become blessings He can use through us. That's just what God intended.

If you work hard for your money and are rewarded, you can appreciate God's gift and use it for blessing. Then you'll have done right and won't be the only one who rejoices.

Legacies

What profit is there in my blood, when I go down to the pit?
Shall the dust praise thee? shall it declare thy truth?
PSALM 30:9

Most people want to be well remembered when they die. We want to leave a legacy of some kind. What will our legacy be? Will it be money or a building or a statue? Will it be something that will last a short while and be gone? Why can't we leave something truly important?

The greatest legacy we can leave is a life well lived. As Christians, we need to be examples of how wonderful Christ can be. We can honestly usher in the kingdom of God on earth if we will devote ourselves to leading kingdom lives. There is profit in the blood of a Christian. Christ's own blood was shed that we might all inherit eternal life. If God was willing to shed His own blood for us, should we be willing to do any less? God's legacy to us is life eternal. What will our legacy to others be?

May each day I live be considered a gift, Father.
Guide me so that I can live each gift to the fullest.
Let others see You through me, I pray. Amen.

Prayers of Thanks

Lord, I thank You that I can have a calm spirit—because You are the Prince of Peace. Your name, Jesus, has the authority to make fear and worry flee. Your name has power! You are called Wonderful Counselor because You freely give wisdom and guidance. You are the Mighty God, the One who made the entire world and keeps it all going. My Everlasting Father, it's Your love and compassion that sustain me. I worship and honor You.

And he will be called Wonderful Counselor,
Mighty God, Everlasting Father, Prince of Peace.
ISAIAH 9:6 NIV

Lord, I am so grateful that I know You—and I am learning more about Your character every day. You are holy and sovereign and righteous and just. You are loving and faithful and always good. When I know the One I believe and have a strong conviction that He is willing and able to help me, I can have more peace. You *want* to help me! My God will take care of me. Thank You, Lord.

I know whom I have believed, and am convinced
that he is able to guard what I have
entrusted to him for that day.
2 TIMOTHY 1:12 NIV

Breath of Life

By the word of the LORD were the heavens made;
and all the host of them by the breath of his mouth.
PSALM 33:6

With a simple breath—inhale and exhale—the Lord brought magnificence into creation. The stars and planets that revolve through space came forth on the breath of the Lord. The hosts, heavenly and earthly, sprang from His mouth. Our world and every last thing in it came into being by His Word. How can the splendor and mystery of our God ever be denied? Our Lord is above all things, and there is nothing that is beyond His control. His breath is within us: the breath of all life. Rejoice!

Creator, Your imagination has yielded wonders beyond comprehension. We stand in awe before Your mighty power. Thank You for finding a place in all of this for me. Your love shines forth throughout all of Your creation. Praise be unto You! Amen.

Heaven on Earth

There is a river, the streams whereof shall
make glad the city of God, the holy place
of the tabernacles of the most High.
PSALM 46:4

In the woods of Maine, not too far from the eastern coast, there is a river that flows clear and cool. It winds through some of the most gorgeous scenery imaginable and carries with it a beauty that is unsurpassed. To see such sights convinces a person of the reality of God. God gives us glimpses of heaven here on earth, so that we might long for such a place from the deepest reaches of our hearts. That part of us that carries the seed of God responds to His beauty in creation. If we look at the world with our spiritual eyes rather than our physical eyes, we will begin to see God's glories in many new ways. The gifts of God are indeed abundant. Open your eyes and enjoy them all.

I stand in awe of the wonder of Your creation, God. Help me to see
beauty wherever I look. Don't let me waste time on ugliness,
but turn my attention to what is good. Amen.

The Real Thing

For a day in thy courts is better than a thousand.
I had rather be a doorkeeper in the house of my God,
than to dwell in the tents of wickedness.
PSALM 84:10

Mike had seen pictures of most of the places he visited before he went. Even so, he was not prepared for the beauty he found. Pictures failed to show the magnitude somehow. Traveling across the country brought everything into sharp focus. Being in it was a thousand times better than just seeing pictures of it.

Nothing beats the real thing. Once we are touched by the grace of God, nothing else compares. What this world has to offer us is but a snapshot of what we can really have. The real thing is best. Embrace God and all that He is and all that He does. You'll never need anything else.

Lord, nothing can compare with You. In my life
I have experienced wonderful things, but none so wonderful
as Your love. Thank You. Amen.

Reasons to Give Thanks

THE INNOCENCE OF CHILDREN
But Jesus said, Suffer little children,
and forbid them not, to come unto me:
for of such is the kingdom of heaven.
MATTHEW 19:14

PEACEFUL SLEEP
I will both lay me down in peace, and sleep: for thou, LORD,
only makest me dwell in safety.
PSALM 4:8

TEARS EXPRESSING OUR JOY OR GRIEF
They that sow in tears shall reap in joy.
PSALM 126:5

Don't Forget the Source

When you have eaten and are satisfied, praise the
LORD your God for the good land he has given you.
DEUTERONOMY 8:10 NIV

God cared for His people throughout their journey to the Promised Land. Whatever trials they faced, they came through with His help, though they sometimes failed to recognize that truth. Whether it was manna in the desert or clothes that lasted for forty years, He never let them lack for anything they truly needed.

As the Israelites came to the Promised Land, God knew that all the good things they'd find there would distract them from Him. When the food required their own efforts, instead of coming directly from His hand, they'd be inclined to believe it resulted only from their planting and harvesting the crop. They'd forget who provided rain and made the plants grow. So God reminded them that thanks were in order when they ate. Everything really came from the same God who'd brought them out of the wilderness into this rich land.

It's the same with us. When we face lean times and have to pray for every meal, we appreciate God's faithfulness. When the paycheck is slim, we clearly see that God has provided for the rent, the heat, and our clothes. But when our paychecks grow or our investments show good returns, it's easy to forget God is still providing. No matter where the money or food comes from, the same Lord provides.

A Joyful Noise

I will be glad and rejoice in You; I will
sing praise to Your name, O Most High.
PSALM 9:2 NKJV

Did you know that God doesn't care how good your singing voice is—He still loves to hear it lifted in praise? Whether you're another Luciano Pavarotti or can't carry a tune in a bucket, God rejoices in the praises of His people, and that includes you!

So don't worry how you sound when you lift up your voice at home or in the church. It doesn't matter if you can't read music or can sight-read perfectly. Don't waste time critiquing yourself or worrying what others think. Instead, rejoice with the psalmist at the wonder of God's love. Even if your neighbors or family don't appreciate your voice, you're really singing to an audience of one: God. And He appreciates every note that shows how much you love Him.

Lord, I praise You! I'm so happy to be Your child,
loved by an omnipotent Father who cares
about the praises I have to offer.

Spiritual Competition?

*I always thank God for you because
of his grace given you in Christ Jesus.*
1 CORINTHIANS 1:4 NIV

When God gives another, younger Christian a great blessing, are you thankful or jealous? Paul felt thankful that a powerful blessing had fallen on the Corinthians. Though they were still young believers and didn't have it all together, the correction Paul administered in his letter to them was not done from a sense of jealousy. A few years later, the apostle let them know he wasn't interested in making himself famous, but in lifting up Jesus. From one who had worked to develop thriving churches on two continents, his sense of humility is amazing.

God doesn't give any of us blessings to start a game of "Who Can Top This?" Realizing the futility of such desires, Paul committed himself to doing the real job—reaching people for Jesus—instead of trying to make himself look good.

Is there a new Christian in your church who's doing great things for God, even though he doesn't know the scriptures as well as you do? Come alongside him and encourage him. Offer to help him however you can. Make it a priority to pray for him. Then thank God for the blessings He's given you, too, and make the most of your gifts, so that together you can lead people to Jesus.

In His Footsteps

Then they said to her, "Woman, why are you weeping?"
She said to them, "Because they have taken away my Lord,
and I do not know where they have laid Him."
JOHN 20:13 NKJV

Faithful Mary Magdalene didn't quite understand. Still she looked for Jesus' body. To her, the Master's disappearance must have seemed one big hoax, perhaps the work of the religious leaders who wanted to get rid of Him any way they could.

The alternative did seem pretty preposterous. What man who died that kind of painful criminal's death came back to life? Crucifixion was a particularly nasty way to end your life, and for that reason, people who died that way were not considered blessed by God. Jesus seemed to be the last person who would receive life again.

Sometimes the people God saves seem to be in the same situation. The "nice" folks we'd love to see come to Him don't. But that onetime biker or gang member does. God doesn't deal in the probabilities that something will be true or false. He works in His own way. What seems impossible one day is a glorious fact the next.

That's the way it was when Jesus was raised from death into new life. We only follow in His footsteps.

Thank You, Lord, for bringing one as impossible
as I to new life. I glory in Your work in my life.

Prayers of Thanks

Lord, I am thankful for the financial resources with which You have blessed me. I want to be a good steward, a wise manager, of the resources You have entrusted to me. Help me to save and spend with discernment and to give to others in need. Help me to find balance—not be a hoarder or an out-of-control spender. Give me a godly view of money and show me how to use it in ways that will honor You.

Now it is required that those who have
been given a trust must prove faithful.
1 CORINTHIANS 4:2 NIV

Lord, I thank You for Your blessings. Whether in plenty or with little, I want to be a cheerful giver. I desire to give from a full heart that serves, not reluctantly or with complaining. I long to see Your money used in ways that will bless others—through my tithing at church or giving to mission organizations or helping the needy. I choose to give at whatever level I can—and ask You to bless it.

Each man should give what he has decided in his
heart to give, not reluctantly or under compulsion,
for God loves a cheerful giver.
2 CORINTHIANS 9:7 NIV

He Chose You

And the blood shall be to you for a token upon the houses where ye are: and when I see the blood, I will pass over you, and the plague shall not be upon you to destroy you, when I smite the land of Egypt.
EXODUS 12:13

On Passover, the Jews did as God commanded and painted the blood of a lamb on their doorposts and lintel. He had promised them that when the angel of death went through Egypt killing the firstborn children and animals, any house having such a mark would be passed by.

Like those ancient Jews, we too have been passed over, though not through the blood of a sheep. The blood shed for us was much more precious—that of God's Son. Where the lamb's blood saved only one nation, Jesus' blood has touched people throughout the world, from every nation and tribe imaginable—including ours.

While we deserved death, God has passed by us because of His Son. Are we awed by that truth? Has it changed the way we live, work, and act? If not, have we asked ourselves, "Out of the whole world, why would God choose me?" If that does not humble us, do we know what Jesus' death means?

*Lord, I'm amazed that you had such mercy on me.
Thank You for Your gift of life.*

Stop and Give Thanks

*"Go out of the ark, you and your wife,
and your sons' wives with you."*
GENESIS 8:16 NKJV

Hearing these words must have ranked as one of the most wonderful moments in Noah's life. A praise party probably followed Noah's announcement that it was time to leave behind their cruise ship and step again on dry land.

The first thing Noah did once they and the animals had left the ark was to build an altar and worship God. How many levels of appreciation he must have felt: first, for the safety of him, his family, and the animals; then gratitude that they could finally leave what by then must have been a very smelly, noisy place. How Noah and family must have looked forward to their new life.

When we come to a happy turning point in our lives, do we rush to thank God? Or do we assume that our own abilities have brought us this far and take the credit for ourselves? We've never stepped foot on an ark, but He's surely cared for us, too.

*Thank You, Lord, for every time You've saved me
and kept me from harm. I praise You for being the
compassionate One who guides my life each day.*

Jesus Doesn't Forget

*And Samuel said unto Jesse, Are here all thy children? And he said,
There remaineth yet the youngest, and, behold, he keepeth the sheep.
And Samuel said unto Jesse, Send and fetch him: for we will not sit
down till he come hither.*
1 SAMUEL 16:11

None of us likes to be forgotten or thought of as unimportant. Even though we may deny it and like to be thought of as independent, others' opinions count to us. We want people to respect our ideas and even seek them out. When there's an honor to be handed out, we'd like to be considered for it, whether it's a promotion or an award.

But even King David had a time when he was forgotten. Out watching sheep—a lowly job—David was out of the way. When the prophet Samuel asked Jesse to see his sons, the father forgot his youngest son. Who would imagine this boy as a king? No one in the family saw the promise in the youth who became a successful warrior and ruler.

Just because others don't see your promise, don't give up. God sees when others are blinded by their humanity. His wonderful, promise-filled future does not rely on human ideas of your value.

Even if the whole world forgets or ignores you, Jesus doesn't.

*Lord, thank You for remembering
me when the world forgets.*

Reasons to Give Thanks

TWO HANDS TO PERFORM TASKS

Whatsoever thy hand findeth to do, do it with thy might;
for there is no work, nor device, nor knowledge, nor wisdom,
in the grave, whither thou goest.
ECCLESIASTES 9:10

LAUGHTER TO EXPRESS OUR JOY

Then was our mouth filled with laughter, and our tongue
with singing: then said they among the heathen,
The LORD hath done great things for them.
PSALM 126:2

THE ACT OF FORGIVENESS

And be ye kind one to another, tenderhearted,
forgiving one another, even as God for Christ's
sake hath forgiven you.
EPHESIANS 4:32

His Hand in Everything

*In every thing give thanks: for this is the will
of God in Christ Jesus concerning you.*
1 THESSALONIANS 5:18

Busy days are best organized by God. Over and over, that truth becomes apparent when you offer up your day to God and a light appears at the end of the tunnel for a seemingly impossible problem. By the end of the day, you've accomplished a lot.

But when the day works out because you've prayed briefly (though perhaps frequently), do you take the credit for yourself, thinking, *I'm glad I worked it all out*, or do you recognize why it worked out in the end and thank the One who smoothed the way for you?

Not thanking God is a terrible oversight—and one that may be very easy to do. Remembering to thank God in an impossible situation, as when a friend or loved one is so ill the doctors can't help, isn't hard. We recognize our limitations and quickly thank Him when we hear the good news of healing. But a heart that's open to Him gradually recognizes His hand in everything, even the small things.

So when your day goes better than expected, thank Him. He's always glad to hear words from a grateful heart.

*Lord, thank You for making every day a better one.
Just knowing You eases my entire life.*

Depend on God

Have mercy upon me, O LORD; for I am weak:
O LORD, heal me; for my bones are vexed.
PSALM 6:2

The closer we get to God, the more glaring are our faults. The brighter the light of perfection, the more flaws are revealed. The better we understand the awesome magnificence of God, the more we expose our own imperfections. As the great men and women of the Bible came to realize, the stronger we become in the faith, the more wretched we sometimes feel.

This, however, is no cause for despair. Our Lord wants nothing more than for us to come to depend on Him. We can only truly become dependent as we acknowledge our inadequacies. As the apostle Paul found out, true strength comes from admitting our weakness, and total healing comes by realizing that without God we are sickly and terminally diseased by sin. Cry out for the mercy of God, and He will strengthen you; ask for His healing, and you will be made whole.

Dear Lord, I try to be perfect and find that I am hopelessly deficient. Nothing I can do will bring me the perfection you intend for me. Fill me with Your Spirit, and do for me all that I cannot do for myself.
Amen.

We Need Each Other

*He poureth contempt upon princes, and causeth them
to wander in the wilderness, where there is no way.*
PSALM 107:40

I don't need any help. I can do everything just fine on my own!"
Randy shouldered his pack and headed down the path. Jerry
and Tom shook their heads and followed. Before long, Randy was
out of sight, and his two friends gave up trying to follow. As evening
set in, they made camp and waited for their friend to return. While
they sat by a warm and inviting fire, Randy stumbled through the
dense forest, lost, alone, and afraid.

We were created for one another. There is no sense in trying to
deny it. Those who attempt to stand on their own two feet find that
they tire before long, and they wish they had someone to lean on.
God created us equal, so that we can adequately fill one another's
needs. He hopes we will share our lives with one another and with
Him. People who feel they are above needing others will be shown
the error of their ways in due time. It is better to admit our need and
wander this wilderness with companions who make the journey a
lot more enjoyable.

*Father, I thank You that I never have to walk alone.
You are by my side, and I have opportunities to
share my life journey with so many others.
Bless my path, O Lord. Amen.*

A Time of Blessing

*And I have given you a land for which ye
did not labour, and cities which ye built not,
and ye dwell in them; of the vineyards and
oliveyards which ye planted not do ye eat.*
JOSHUA 24:13

Sometimes things come easily to us. The work seems to go smoothly, and the rewards seem even larger than we expected. *What, am I on a roll?* we may want to ask ourselves.

No, it's not a roll, it's a time of blessing. Sometimes God just seems to let us have so much, we wonder why He's doing it. Life seems wonderful, and we can enjoy it. But we can't forget that all this blessing has a purpose. God doesn't give a promotion without expecting we'll use our new position wisely. He doesn't give raises that He expects us to spend only on ourselves; we need to remember the work of His church and give accordingly.

Feeling blessed? Have you asked God what you can do to share that blessing? Then have you done what He commanded?

*Thank You, Lord, for the many blessings
You've given me. Today show me how to
use the ones in my hand now.*

Prayers of Thanks

Lord, I thank You for my wonderful friends! As I think about the treasure chest of my close friends, casual friends, and acquaintances, I am grateful for the blessings and the joys each one brings to my life. Thank You for my close friends—those who listen, care, and encourage me. I acknowledge that You, Lord, are the giver of all good gifts, and I thank You for Your provision in my friendships.

> *A man of many companions may come to ruin,*
> *but there is a friend who sticks closer than a brother.*
> PROVERBS 18:24 NIV

Lord, I thank You for my family members and those who are like family to me. I am grateful for their love and understanding. May I be loving in return—not only with those who love me, but even with those who are hard to be around. Your ways are merciful and kind, forgiving and good. Help me to reflect Your love, finding joy in loving others as You love me.

> *"If you love those who love you, what reward will you get?*
> *Are not even the tax collectors doing that?"*
> MATTHEW 5:46 NIV

Power from God

"Let him who boasts boast in the Lord."
1 CORINTHIANS 1:31 NIV

Are you on a spiritual high? Is life going well for you at home, at the workplace, and in a ministry? Then you may be in a very dangerous place. You may feel tempted to take credit for all those good things. Perhaps you're starting to feel as if you have some special spiritual knowledge that makes you better than others. Or maybe you've reached out to others, they've responded to Jesus, and you're starting to feel you're an outrageous witness for God.

It's great that God is using you so powerfully, but don't forget that He's the One giving you the power to speak those words and that it's His Spirit that's touching the hearts. We are tools in God's hands, and we need to be ready for Him to pick up and use us, but we're not the One who made the plans and brought them to completion.

Praise God for your successes, but remember that without Him, they are impossible. Boast about what happened if you want, but boast that Jesus did it, not you.

Lord, I want to lift up Your name so others
know what's happening and who caused it.
I could never do this on my own.

Trust in Him

My soul finds rest in God alone;
my salvation comes from him.
PSALM 62:1 NIV

Whom do you really trust? In this life perhaps you have some good friends and family members who are reliable. Maybe you have a few whom you'd prefer to trust carefully because of their past track records. But David tells us that God was the One he *really* trusted in—the One he could trust even with his soul.

Right now, you may trust that your sister will keep your secret, that your friend will return the garden tools he borrowed, or that your parents will come through with the down payment on a new home. If these things fell through, it would only affect you for a short time. You'd manage something else or get over it. Yet David's trust is not for a few days, weeks, or months, but for eternity. He has hung his heart on the truth that God will save him, both in this world and the next.

Who are you trusting with your soul today? Some people wrongly trust in tarot readers, psychics, and others as they look to the future. Others assertively deny that there is any future after this life. But everyone is trusting in something. Many bank on sliding into an eternal nothingness, but even they trust that there is no eternity. Where are you looking for your eternity?

Lord, let me trust in You alone.

Ticket to Eternity

*Now when a man works, his wages are not credited to
him as a gift, but as an obligation. However, to the man
who does not work but trusts God who justifies the wicked,
his faith is credited as righteousness.*
ROMANS 4:4–5 NIV

You probably don't work for free—you need money to live on,
pay the rent with, and save for a rainy day. The scriptures
recognize that a valuable worker deserves fair recompense.

Though the Bible recognizes the need to earn a living, it also
tells us God's kingdom isn't like that. We can't work our way into
heaven, because we can't do anything to make ourselves right with
God. The only one who can do that is God's perfect Son, Jesus.
When we believe that He died in order to forgive our sins, we
agree with God on the subject, and our eternal destination becomes
heaven. God gives us that gift for doing nothing more than trusting
in Him.

Spend time today in worship; and instead of trying to enter
heaven on your own credit, you'll arrive there safely on your trust in
Jesus. It's the only way you *can* get in.

*Thank You, Lord, that I can only enter into heaven
by trusting in You. I could work 24/7 and never
build up the righteousness You offer as a gift.*

Reasons to Give Thanks

FREEDOM OF WORSHIP
I will worship toward thy holy temple,
and praise thy name.
PSALM 138:2

BEAUTIFUL MUSIC TO ENJOY
Sing unto him a new song;
play skillfully with a loud noise.
PSALM 33:3

THE WARMTH OF A FIRE IN WINTER
I will praise thee, O LORD, with my whole heart;
I will shew forth all thy marvelous works.
PSALM 9:1

Heavenly Party

*I say unto you, that likewise joy shall be in heaven
over one sinner that repenteth, more than over ninety
and nine just persons, which need no repentance.*
LUKE 15:7

H as God ever thrown a party for you? Do you know how much doing that would thrill Him?

When a soul enters eternity by faith in Jesus, all heaven rejoices over that new member of God's kingdom. You might say God throws a party just for the new believer. All heaven celebrates for each person who comes to God through His Son. If you know Jesus, there was a day when God gave a celebration with your name on it. Invitations went out to all heaven, and everyone had a great time rejoicing in what God had done in your life. It was a great day!

If you've never had such a great day in your life, it can still happen. All you need to do is admit to God that you need to turn your life around. Tell Him you know you've sinned and need His forgiveness and that you're trusting in Jesus for that forgiveness.

Do you hear a party starting?

*Lord, thank You that all heaven rejoices at the salvation of one person.
Thank You that You were willing to let all heaven celebrate
because I came to faith in You. Amen.*

Reason for Praise

Let everything that has breath praise the LORD.
PSALM 150:6 NKJV

W hy is the Bible always telling us to praise God? Is He really stuck on Himself? Or does He need praise to feel good about Himself? Instead, why doesn't God tell us to praise one another— or even share some of our own wonderful qualities with others? Doesn't He like us very much?

These questions are actually pretty silly once you realize the kind of God you're talking about. He does not desire praise because He's a weakling. Instead, He tells us to praise Him because by doing that, our hearts recognize His infinite greatness and powerfulness. Only by praise can we recognize who He is and how small we are in comparison. Praise opens our eyes to God's true character. With it we can voice how much we appreciate the world He created for us, the love He freely gives, and the thousands of other graces He offers us.

As we comprehend God's greatness, we more completely appreciate His mercy and love in sending us Jesus. Through Jesus, the all-powerful One stepped into our world and became one of us, though He already owned the entire universe and didn't have to respond.

He only took that step so that He could also own our hearts.

In God's Image

*So God created man in his own image, in the image of God
created he him; male and female created he them.*
GENESIS 1:27

"We hold these truths to be self-evident that all men are
created equal," wrote Thomas Jefferson in the Declaration of
Independence. Try to write those words in a government document
today, and you'd probably take some flak; but Jefferson had no
problem in his day, because even those like himself who were not
committed Christians accepted certain facts about God. Though
Jefferson himself did not believe in all the scripture, he surely
accepted creation as fact.

What wise men accepted several hundred years ago is now
doubted by so many. But that has not changed the truth. You *are*
created in God's image. Whether you are male or female, He values
you deeply. And from Him you have the promise of a potential that
goes far beyond your own meager skills and abilities.

Don't let those who doubt discourage you from believing what
many of our founding fathers accepted without question. God did
make you. You are valuable to Him and "endowed with inalienable
rights." Better than the "life, liberty, and the pursuit of happiness"
Jefferson propounded, God offers you life eternal with Him.

Willing Children

When I consider thy heavens, the work of thy fingers,
the moon and the stars, which thou hast ordained; what is man,
that thou art mindful of him?
PSALM 8:3–4

A devout man refused to enter a church because he said that he was not worthy to tread on holy ground. Whenever he saw a cross, he burst into tears and turned his eyes away, lamenting that he would never be good enough to hope for salvation.

One day a traveling minister entered the man's hometown. He saw the devout man sitting on the stones outside the church building, and so he stopped to talk. When he found out the man's thoughts, he told him, "God is not looking for worthy men, but willing children. He doesn't want to be surrounded by people trying to impress Him with how much they can love Him. He merely wants people who will receive the great love He has to give. Come, and receive the gift of the Lord. He set the earth and skies in motion, the birds in the air, the fish in the sea, the creatures on the earth; and He did it all for you, my friend."

Though I do not deserve Your great love, Father God, I thank You that
You give it so freely. Embrace me as a child, cradle me in Your strong
and tender arms, and help me remember that I am Yours. Amen.

Prayers of Thanks

I praise You, Lord, thanking You for this great nation. You have blessed America! Thank You for peace. Thank You for the freedom to speak and be heard and to vote for our leaders. Help us to uphold godly values as we seek to honor the authority of those who govern our land. Please keep the United States united—as one strong country that seeks Your face and favor.

Give thanks to the LORD, call on his name;
make known among the nations what he has done.
PSALM 105:1 NIV

Lord, I thank You for all the men and women serving in our armed forces. They choose to put their lives on the line so we can have freedom and peace—and for that I am truly grateful. Protect them and keep them safe. Comfort them and give them strength when they are away from loved ones. Bless, too, the families who send soldiers to war or for duty overseas. I pray that You would meet their every need, Lord.

The LORD is my strength and my shield;
my heart trusts in him, and I am helped.
PSALM 28:7 NIV

In Control

Jumping up, they mobbed him and forced him to the edge of the hill on which the town was built. They intended to push him over the cliff, but he passed right through the crowd and went on his way.
LUKE 4:29–30 NLT

The people in Jesus' hometown of Nazareth were so angry at Him, they wanted to kill Him. In fact, they took Him to a cliff to throw Him over. A few more minutes, and if He hadn't been God's Son, He would've been history.

But did you miss the most important part of those verses? Jesus just slips away. An irate mob, and He just walks through it as if it were water. No one stops Him. No one questions Him. In a few minutes, He's on His way. Jesus' whole life—and death—was under God's control. Nothing could touch Him until the Father okayed it. No one could harm Him without God's permission.

That's true of God's children, too. When trouble comes our way, God hasn't lost control. He's in that situation with us, guiding our steps and sharing our sorrow. Don't forget the many times you've slipped through the crowd, as God has smoothed the way and made life simpler. He's saved you from harm because He had another plan, and a cliff wasn't in it. He's in control, no matter what happens.

Lord, whatever happens to me,
I'm glad You're in control.

True Kindness

A gift is as a precious stone in the eyes of him that hath it:
withersoever it turneth, it prospereth.
PROVERBS 17:8

The rain was coming down in sheets now, and she had no idea how to change a flat. As long as it was raining so hard, she held out little hope of getting someone to stop and help her. Suddenly she heard a tap on her window.

"Need some help?"

"I've got a flat, and I don't know how to fix it."

"You go wait with my wife in my car, and I'll have it changed in a jiffy."

Her savior was a young man with a beard and a kind face. He worked quickly in the pouring rain, and when he was finished he was drenched to the bone. She thanked him and began to pull a twenty-dollar bill out of her wallet, but he refused to take it.

"Do something nice for someone else, and we'll call it square," he said.

True kindness doesn't look for any rewards. It is done from the heart, and there is no payment great enough to cover it. It is only when we learn from it and then give it to someone else that kindness is repaid. Giving of ourselves to others is a precious gift, and when we give it, it just keeps on going.

Help me to give kindness, love, and care, Father.
Bless my effort, that my gift may grow and spread. Amen.

Abundant Life

"The thief comes only to steal and kill and destroy;
I have come that they may have life, and have it to the full."
JOHN 10:10 NIV

A bundant life, full of good things on this earth, spiritual peace and joy, and full, satisfying relationships—that's what God intends His people to have. But listen to the world, and you'd never know it. Non-Christians often portray Christians as narrow-minded, sad, or hopelessly idealistic.

Your life in Jesus is probably nothing like that. When your faith is alive and active, you can feel clean, right with your Maker, and richer for being in a relationship with Him. He's been working in your life to bring spiritual abundance, deeper understanding of Him and the world around you, and joy that doesn't stop when trouble enters the door.

Nonbelievers can't know any of that. You can tell them that loving Jesus is the best thing ever, and they may think you're crazy. They've never experienced anything like it, so they can't imagine such peace and joy.

But one day the thief who came to steal, kill, and destroy their lives may make them so miserable that God's message can enter a crack in their armor against Him. They start to listen to His message of abundant life. Before long faith blossoms, and new life—abundant life—takes hold.

It's time to rejoice in Jesus.

Reasons to Give Thanks

THE LOVE OF FAMILY

And I will bless them that bless thee, and curse
him that curseth thee: and in thee shall all
families of the earth be blessed.
GENESIS 12:3

TRUE FRIENDS WHO ARE THERE
REGARDLESS OF CIRCUMSTANCES

A friend loveth at all times.
PROVERBS 17:17

GOD'S WORD, THE BREAD OF LIFE

It is written, that man shall not live by bread alone,
but by every word of God.
LUKE 4:4

God's Friend

"But you, O Israel, my servant, Jacob, whom I have chosen, you
descendants of Abraham my friend, I took you from the ends of the
earth, from its farthest corners I called you. I said, 'You are my servant';
I have chosen you and have not rejected you."
ISAIAH 41:8–9 NIV

Have you pondered the idea that, like Israel, the Lord of the universe is your friend? Perhaps you've been stopped in your tracks by the awe of that truth. *Why should He care for me?* you may wonder.

God chooses His friends on His own terms. The famous, the extraordinarily intelligent, the powerful aren't always on His list. Yet some of the most unexpected folks are. He doesn't choose based on worldly greatness. His own sense of mercy defines the choice in ways we cannot now understand.

Many blessings follow friendship with God, but so do challenges. The Creator expects much of His friends, just as He gives much. Being a friend of Jesus requires that we suffer, struggle, and face numerous challenges, physical and spiritual. It's not the kind of thing He offers lightly or that we should accept blindly.

But when God chooses a friend, it's for forever. He never gives up or changes His mind. He's with you for this lifetime and eternity. Along with all the purely delightful things in His hand, He offers strength in trials and guidance for a long, hard way.

That's the best friendship anyone could offer.

Brimming with His Spirit

May God give you more and more mercy,
peace, and love.
JUDE 2 NLT

What a blessing, to continually receive more and more of God's mercy, peace, and love. That's just the kind of Christian life we'd like to have—until we're bursting with these good spiritual experiences, to the point where we simply can't hold them in.

Maybe we have already received so much from God. Our lives have changed drastically because of the salvation He offered. But bursting? Perhaps we wouldn't use *that* word to describe ourselves.

That's because God doesn't overfill us with His blessings. He gives us enough to share then waits to see what we do with it. God gives blessings so we can encourage, teach, and lead others into a relationship with Him. He doesn't give them so that we can bulge with His unused gifts.

But if we receive God's gifts and pass them on to others, take hold of His Word and teachings, and use them to show others how to live, God fills us again.

When we've made that our lifestyle, we are truly blessed—and so are others who come in contact with us. Their growth in turn touches others' lives—and on and on it goes. The joys of mercy, peace, and love abound, just as God planned.

God Provides

Honour the LORD with thy substance, and with
the firstfruits of all thine increase: So shall thy
barns be filled with plenty, and thy presses
shall burst out with new wine.
PROVERBS 3:9–10

A poor woman approached two men asking for money to buy bread for her children. The first man scowled and said, "I work hard for my money. Go and do the same for yourself and for your family!" The woman began to walk away, but the other man stopped her and said, "Poor woman, take this money, for it is not really mine. I do work hard for it, but it is by God's grace that I have it at all. If I give to you, I simply give to God what He has provided."

It is good to remember that without God we would not possess the things we do. All things come to us from God, and it is good that we share them. Jesus tells us that whenever we come to the aid of another person in need, we are in fact aiding Him. True prosperity comes only when we learn to give to others as freely as God gives to us.

Oh Father, soften my heart to those who are less fortunate than I am.
Help me to appreciate the blessings I have been given and to share
from my abundance. Amen.

Real Wisdom

Counsel is mine, and sound wisdom:
I am understanding; I have strength.
PROVERBS 8:14

Solomon was considered to be the wisest of all human beings. His judgment was sound and fair. Subjects traveled from all over Israel to seek his counsel. His word was law because people believed there was no greater mind in all the world. Solomon did nothing more than use the gifts God had given him in the best way possible. He prayed long and hard for God to inspire him with special wisdom.

Solomon was able to give great wisdom because he was in touch with the source of wisdom: God. As much as Solomon was willing to give himself to God, God was willing to give Himself right back. God showed that He was willing to do the same for us by giving Himself in the person of His Son, Jesus Christ. All we need to do is accept His gift and try to the best of our ability to follow His example. Like Solomon, we receive strength and understanding from the God who gives us all good things.

Lord, I wish I could be one with Your Spirit, that I might spread Your will in this world. You offer so much, and I take so little. Help me to use what You hold forth, that I might reflect the blessed light of Your Son, Jesus Christ, throughout this world. Amen.

Thank You, God, for Everything

Thank You, God, for everything—
the big things and the small—
For every good gift comes from God,
the giver of them all.
And so at this time we offer up a prayer
To thank You, God, for giving us
a lot more than our share.
First, thank You for the little things
that often come our way—
The things we take for granted
and don't mention when we pray—
The unexpected courtesy, the thoughtful, kindly deed,
A hand reached out to help us
in the time of sudden need.
Then thank You for the miracles
we are much too blind to see,
and give us new awareness
of our many gifts from Thee.
And help us to remember that the key to life and living
Is to make each prayer a prayer of thanks
and each day a day of thanksgiving.

HELEN STEINER RICE

Who to Thank

Give thanks unto the LORD, call upon his name, make known
his deeds among the people. Sing unto him, sing psalms unto him,
talk ye of all his wondrous works.
1 CHRONICLES 16:8–9

Is Thanksgiving a joyful time for you? It can be if you're focused on the One who deserves your thanks. But often we become so wrapped up in a large turkey dinner, a family get-together, and other holiday celebrations that we lose our joy.

Though the Pilgrims have been stereotyped as sour-faced folks, that image is wrong. When they had a successful harvest in 1621, they just had to rejoice. Some men went out to shoot game for their harvest celebration table, and the Pilgrims invited the Wampanoag Indians. Their celebration lasted three days. Though no formal religious service was part of the first celebration, Edward Winslow, who wrote a letter to England about it, reported that it was by God's goodness that the small band of Christians was far from want. They knew who to thank.

So make Thanksgiving a time of joy when you remember the blessings of God. Whether you're joining a large family or celebrating alone, it's a time to remember the love that's brought you to this point in your life.

Say one big "thanks" to God.

Thank You, Lord, for the blessing of Your love.
Keep me faithful in thanks all year long.

Give Thanks

*Powerful Prayers for
Everyday Blessings*

CONTENTS

INTRODUCTION

Perhaps one of the most difficult Christian teachings to put into practice comes from Paul in his first letter to the Thessalonians: "Rejoice always; pray without ceasing; in everything give thanks."

At face value, it seems like a simple command to carry out. After all, it's so easy to give joyful thanks for the big, obvious blessings that our generous God has bestowed on us—our families, our homes, our freedom, and our prosperity. But how often do we send up praise for the unassuming gifts of laundry, traffic jams, and laugh lines? In their own way, these blessings in disguise truly reveal the nonstop, intimate nature of the love our Father seeks to shower upon His beloved children. But every day we overlook a multitude of God's richest gifts, taking them for granted and writing them off as inconvenient and mundane.

This book is designed to challenge you to open your eyes and recognize the praiseworthy blessings that are around every corner. Divided into convenient sections for browsing, you'll find prayers on everything from the express checkout line and sleepless nights to daylight savings time and bathroom scales—all offering a joyful new perspective that will leave you in awe of our God's marvelous goodness.

So don't waste another moment—*Give Thanks!*

The Daily Grind

Finding the miraculous in the mundane

Paper Cuts

• • • • • •

Father, it's amazing that something as small as
a paper cut can be so painful. Thank You for
this reminder that when one part of the body
is in pain, the whole body suffers. Help me stay
positive and apply this principle to my daily life.

Budgeting Wisely

• • • • • •

Lord, there are so many ways to spend money
that it can be overwhelming, but I thank You
for giving me so many choices. Thank You for
the promise of wisdom when I ask for it and for
entrusting this money to me. Help me spend it in
a way that honors You.

Learning a New Skill

• • • • • •

Father, it's hard to learn a new skill. I sometimes
feel inept and unable when I try something new.
Thank You for the gift of patience as I learn. I am
grateful that You have given me everything I need
to succeed.

Facing a Learning Challenge

• • • • • •

Dear Father, I feel frustrated when I cannot do something I think I should be able to do. It's times like these when I am most grateful for the special talents and abilities You have given especially to me. Thank You for Your calming presence. Help me slow down and trust that all things are possible through You.

Since everything God created is good,
we should not reject any of it
but receive it with thanks.
1 TIMOTHY 4:4 NLT

Sick with a Cold

• • • • • •

Lord, I hate being sick. How could I ever take feeling well for granted? I'm miserable right now, but I know I'll be back to normal soon. Thank You for creating my body with the blessed ability to heal itself.

Working Out

• • • • • •

Lord, today is one of those days when the couch is looking a whole lot more tempting than my workout routine. . . . Sometimes it's hard to get motivated, but I know regular exercise will honor my body—Your temple. Thank You for giving me a body that is so fearfully and wonderfully made and the awesome responsibility that comes with it.

First Day of School

• • • • • •

Lord, the first day can be so intimidating. As a new school year begins, help me set goals with You in mind. Despite the uncertainty, I am thankful for this opportunity to begin anew and learn in abundance.

Going to the Dentist

• • • • • •

Father, I certainly dread all those instruments and drills. But as much as I dislike going to the dentist, I know it's a necessary discomfort that I would be at a loss without. Thank You for making dental care available to me, and give me the resolve to take advantage of it.

The LORD directs the steps of the godly.
He delights in every detail of their lives.
PSALM 37:23 NLT

A New Boss

* * * * * *

Lord, adjusting to a new boss isn't always easy,
and though I may be apprehensive, I thank You
for this new leader. Thank You for all the people
of authority You have placed in my life. Help me
follow their guidance and make this person's job
easier by doing mine well.

A New Coworker

* * * * * *

Father, thank You for a new coworker. I know our
paths have not crossed by accident. As I get to
know them, help me share with them Your light
and Your love.

Turning Off the Lights
for the Night

• • • • • •

Heavenly Father, another day is done. Thank You
for the things I accomplished today with Your
help, and thank You for abiding with me as I
sleep.

First Day Back from Vacation

• • • • • •

Lord, as hard as it is to come back from vacation,
thank You for the time to rest, relax, and
rejuvenate. Thank You for a routine to come back
to. Thank You for the importance You place on
rest and for continuing to guide me in making it
a priority.

Rejoice always; pray without ceasing;
in everything give thanks; for this is
God's will for you in Christ Jesus.
1 THESSALONIANS 5:16–18 NASB

111

April 15

* * * * * *

Dear Father, paying taxes often feels like an enormous burden, but help me to be grateful for the blessings my tax dollars provide—good roads, libraries, education. Thank You for the privileges of living in a wealthy country.

Standing in Line at the DMV

* * * * * *

Lord, when it comes to standing in line, the line at the DMV has to be the longest. Thank You for the gift of patience, and help me keep this time spent waiting in perspective. It's such a privilege to be able to transport myself from one place to another, and this is but a small price to pay for that freedom.

While on Hold

* * * * * *

I have such a hard time waiting for things, Lord, but I'm grateful for this reminder that I'm not at the center of the universe—You are. Thank You, Father, for never putting me on hold.

My Third Cup of Coffee

· · · · · ·

Thank heaven for coffee! It's definitely a three-
cup kind of day, Father. . . . Help my body utilize
this caffeine and focus on the task at hand.

*Don't worry about anything; instead,
pray about everything. Tell God what you need,
and thank him for all he has done.*

PHILIPPIANS 4:6 NLT

Waiting on a Download

· · · · · ·

Father, I've become so spoiled by lightning-fast
results: fast food, instant messages, and high-
speed Internet. Thank You for this technology
that makes my daily life more convenient—
I know it's unreasonable to expect everything
instantaneously. Your triumphant return is
especially worth the wait.

Checking E-Mail

* * * * * *

Sometimes I wish I could just turn off my e-mail, Lord. So many messages! Some days they seem never ending. Deep down, though, I know I'm grateful for this speedy communication—even if it means an extra hour at the office.

No Parking Spots Up Front

* * * * * *

You have blessed me with two capable legs, Lord— so why do I avoid putting them to good use? I dread the spot at the back of the lot, but I know the extra little bit of exercise will benefit me.

When the Day Drags

* * * * * *

Thank You for this uneventful day, Lord. I may feel tempted to steal an anxious glance at the clock, but I'm grateful for every moment, no matter how slowly they seem to pass. I cherish this calm day because only You know what tomorrow will bring.

He calms the storm, so that its waves are still.

PSALM 107:29 NKJV

Running to the Convenience Store

• • • • • •

I can be so forgetful sometimes, Lord!
Though I'm bothered that I need to run back
to the store, I'm grateful that I have convenient
places to turn. In the same way, I'm grateful that I
have You to turn to with my frustrations.
Thanks for always being there for me, Father.

Stuck in Traffic

• • • • • •

Thank You, Lord, for giving me this opportunity
to slow down and stop rushing through life.
Sometimes I need a reminder that it's okay if
things don't go my way. It's Your master plan that
really matters. I may arrive at my destination later
than intended, but I am grateful to have this time
to spend with You.

Road Construction

· · · · · ·

Even though I may perceive road construction as a hassle, Lord, I am thankful for safe roads to drive on. Remind me that the big picture is worth all the detours and delays.

Red Lights and Stop Signs

· · · · · ·

Lord, these delays aren't often welcome, but I know they are necessary to ensure my safety and the safety of everyone else on the road. Help me recognize these moments of pause as quick opportunities to reflect and recharge.

Praise the LORD; I may never forget the good things he does for me. He forgives all my sins and heals all my diseases. He redeems me from death and crowns me with love and tender mercies.

PSALM 103:2–4 NLT

Long To-Do List

• • • • • • •

Dear Jesus, I am overwhelmed. There are many
things on my list to do today. Thank You for
giving me useful work to do, and I pray that Your
priorities would be mine.

Tough to Get Out of Bed

• • • • • •

Lord, it seems the moment I settle in to sleep,
the alarm goes off and it is time to face another
day. Thank You for the hope and brightness of
morning and the promise this new beginning
brings.

Another Day on the Job

• • • • • •

Lord, thank You for this job. Though I don't
always look forward to it, it is a gift from You.
I am grateful for meaningful work to do and a
steady paycheck. Help me to be a light among my
coworkers.

Monday

· · · · · ·

Father, thank You for a new week and a clean slate. I don't always look forward to Mondays, but I am grateful You have given me this day as an opportunity to start new projects and finish old ones. Help me be productive and consistently put You first.

The LORD says, "I will guide you along the best pathway for your life. I will advise you and watch over you."

PSALM 32:8 NLT

A Day of Meetings

· · · · · ·

Father, there are many ways I'd like to spend this day, and sitting in meetings is not one of them, but thank You for sitting here with me. Thank You for a job that provides for my family. Thank You that all meetings eventually come to an end.

Working Late

* * * * * *

Father, it's hard to work late, but I'm thankful
I have a job and work to do. Thank You for an
opportunity to work without interruptions and
for helping me meet this deadline.

New Responsibility

* * * * * *

Lord, I am grateful for being entrusted with this
new responsibility, even though it may mean
more work. Thank You for those people in my life
who trust me with important tasks. With Your
help, I know I won't let them down.

Change

* * * * * *

Lord, thank You for the constancy of change. I
may not always like it, but I know it's a necessary
part of life. Remind me that even when I think
things have changed for the worse, there is always
a blessing to be gained.

Godliness with contentment is great gain.

1 TIMOTHY 6:6 KJV

Home Sweet Home

The blessings at your doorstep

Telemarketers

• • • • • •

Lord, when I think of telemarketers, nothing good comes to mind. Thank You for Your example when it comes to dealing with people I don't like. Though I may groan when the phone rings at dinnertime, I will make a habit of looking to You for guidance and patience.

Spiders in the Garden

• • • • • •

I am in awe of Your creation, Father, and there are few things more exquisite than a dew-laden spiderweb at dawn while I'm pulling weeds—but when it comes to encountering the spiders themselves. . .that's a different story. Help me recognize the beauty and benefits in the creepiest and crawliest of Your amazing creatures. I know my garden would be at a loss without them.

First Dandelion

• • • • • •

Father, the first dandelion is a sure sign that spring is on the way, but I dread its appearance in my lawn. Thank You for this promise of new life, and remind me that You alone are the master of Your creation.

Bird Droppings on the Windshield

• • • • • • •

Lord, sometimes it seems as though the birds know when I've just washed the car. Thank You for Your amazing creations that fly and sing so sweetly throughout the day. Help me keep my frustration in perspective.

This is the day the LORD has made;

let us rejoice and be glad in it.

PSALM 118:24 NIV

Walking the Dog

• • • • • • •

Sometimes taking care of a pet can be a hassle, Lord, but I thank You for this fresh air—this time to get away from the phone, the television, and the doorbell. Thank You for the way this walk energizes me and gives me something productive to do.

Cleaning the Litter Pan

• • • • • •

Cleaning the litter pan is not a task I look
forward to, Father, but my feline companion
is worth it. Thank You for all the joy the furry
friends in my life bring.

Paying the Rent/Mortgage

• • • • • •

Father, thank You for a place to lay my head and
for the warmth and security my home provides.
Thank You for the resources that enable me to
write this check each month.

Hanging Pictures

• • • • • •

Lord, hanging pictures is sometimes tedious.
It can be a chore making sure things are straight
and properly placed. Thank You for the memories
these pictures hold. Thank You for being present
in all the details of my life.

All the days of the afflicted are bad,
but a cheerful heart has a continual feast.
PROVERBS 15:15 NASB

A Messy Closet

• • • • • •

Father, I am grateful to You for blessing me with
the resources to have such a jam-packed closet.
Though I dread cleaning it, guide me in keeping
only what I need and donating the rest to those
who are less fortunate. Thank You for always
meeting my needs—spiritually and physically.

Making the Bed

• • • • • •

I never look forward to having one more thing to
do in the morning, Lord, but I'm glad to have a
warm bed to sleep in when I come home at night.
Help me take pride in the blessings You have
given me.

Brushing My Teeth

• • • • • •

Father, brushing my teeth often feels like just another thing on my morning and nightly to-do list. Though it can be a hassle, I'm grateful that I have access to the necessary resources to care for my body and for the daily opportunity to keep myself healthy.

Changing a Lightbulb

• • • • • •

Changing a lightbulb is such a simple thing but often something I put off and take for granted. Thank You for the blessing of light, and continue to guide me in seeking Your light.

Do not conform any longer to the pattern of this world, but be transformed by the renewing of your mind.

ROMANS 12:2 NIV

Washing Dishes

* * * * * *

Dishpan hands, murky water, stuck toiling away after dinner while everyone else goes about their business. . . Not much to love about washing dishes, Lord. I am grateful, though, for clean running water and being able to wash my dishes so thoroughly and conveniently.

On the Bathroom Scale

* * * * * *

The bathroom scale doesn't lie, Lord. You have blessed me abundantly, and it shows. I am grateful for these few extra pounds—especially when I consider that there are so many less fortunate than me who go hungry every day. Show me how to provide for others as You have so generously provided for me.

Cleaning the Attic/Basement

* * * * * *

Thank You, Lord, for all the memories these boxes hold. As I sift through everything here, help me hang on to my fond memories and let go of the meaningless objects. I am grateful that You have blessed me with such a full life and rich legacy of loved ones.

Folding Laundry

Father, sometimes the laundry seems never ending, but I'm glad this means plenty of clean clothes for me and my family. Thank You for blessing us with a convenient means of washing away the stains of the day and for providing us with clean hearts, too.

Do not be anxious about anything,
but in everything, by prayer and petition,
with thanksgiving, present your requests to God.
And the peace of God, which transcends
all understanding, will guard your hearts.

PHILIPPIANS 4:6–7 NIV

Pouring a Glass of Water

Father, I turn on a faucet at least a dozen times a day, never expecting anything but clean water to come out. I'm grateful I've never had reason to doubt this everyday blessing—or Your awesome love for me. Thank You for the gift of faith.

Scrubbing the Toilet Bowl

* * * * * *

Lord, cleaning the toilet is not a pleasant task, but I am forever grateful for the sanitary conveniences I have available to me. Thank You for blessing me with a clean, healthy environment and the ability to maintain it.

Cleaning the Chimney

* * * * * *

Lord, thank You for all the warm, comforting fires that made this chimney so dirty. I am grateful for Your gift of fire and the warmth of Your everlasting love.

Taking Out the Trash

* * * * * *

Even though this is one of my least favorite chores, Father, I am grateful that You have blessed my family with so many resources that we can afford to dispose of some of them. Help us keep Your creation bright and beautiful by making us mindful of what we throw away.

Offer unto God thanksgiving;
and pay thy vows unto the most High.

PSALM 50:14 KJV

Running a Bath

* * * * * *

Father, it sometimes seems like it takes forever for the bath to fill up—especially when I need one the most. Give me patience to wait for Your blessings. Thank You for abundant water and warm, bubbly relaxation.

Nothing on TV

* * * * * *

Thank You for this opportunity to spend time with my family and do something productive, Lord. I seem to be always seeking someone or something to entertain me. Thank You for blessing me with this free time to focus on others and grow closer to the ones I love.

Turning On the Lights

* * * * * *

Lord, thank You for the things I take for granted every day, like electricity—the flip of a switch, and my world is illuminated. Thank You especially for the light You provide that guides my steps as I go about my day.

Cutting the Grass

* * * * * *

Lord, there is nothing like the smell of freshly cut grass. Thank You for fresh air and exercise. Thank You for the beauty that surrounds me while I work.

*Give thanks in all circumstances,
for this is God's will for you in Christ Jesus.*
1 THESSALONIANS 5:18 NIV

Computer Is Down

• • • • • •

Father, Your Word says to give thanks in all circumstances, even when my computer is down. Thank You for the time to quiet my soul and rest my brain from the constant stream of information.

Deciding What to Fix for Dinner

• • • • • •

Father, in a world where so many are in need, thank You for the luxury of wondering what to fix for dinner. Thank You for the daily bread only You can provide.

Cleaning the Kitchen

• • • • • •

Father, the kitchen is a mess and I'm tired, but thank You for the strength to clean it up. Thank You that messy kitchens (and lots of other messes in my life) are only temporary.

Shoveling Snow

• • • • • •

Father, thank You for the beauty of snow and for endowing me with the strength to move it from my path. Help me always recognize Your beautiful blessings—even if they require a little extra effort to adapt to.

Why art thou cast down, O my soul? and why art thou disquieted within me? hope thou in God: for I shall yet praise him, who is the health of my countenance, and my God.

PSALM 42:11 KJV

Raking Leaves

• • • • • •

Thank You, Father, for the beauty of autumn—for the crisp air and fall colors. Thank You for this exercise and the opportunity to be outdoors. I am so grateful for Your blessings in due season.

Nosy Neighbors

• • • • • •

Thank You, Lord, for neighbors who care about what's going on in my life. I may not always appreciate their attention, but I'm grateful to have people living close by who are looking out for me and my family, just as I am grateful for Your watchful care from above.

Putting Away Christmas Decorations

• • • • • •

Dear Lord, it is such a joy to celebrate Your Son's birth. Thank You for another holiday season to enjoy with my family and friends. Thank You for the memories associated with each item I am packing away for next year. Help me to treasure the things that You do.

Trying a New Recipe

• • • • • •

Lord, thank You for this new recipe. Thank You for the food You've provided and the creativity with which I can prepare it day after day. Thank You for the rich variety and the joy of preparing food for my family and friends.

Cleaning the Gutters

• • • • • •

Father, there is truly no limit to Your blessings. Thank You for providing me with a roof over my head and protection from storms. I rejoice in all Your provisions, great and small.

Crayon on the Wall

• • • • • •

Lord, thank You for creative expression and childhood innocence. Though my first instinct is to be frustrated with the writing on the wall, grant me an understanding and forgiving heart. Help me guide my children in expressing themselves in productive ways that honor You.

Leftovers for Dinner

• • • • • •

Father, I don't always look forward to leftover night, but I'm glad to have the night off from cooking. Thank You for making sure I have everything I need and then some. Help me use this nourishment to do Your will.

Putting Away Spring Clothing

• • • • • •

Dear Jesus, thank You for another season come
and gone. I am in awe of the careful way You craft
one day to the next in a seamless array of beauty
and splendor. Help me recognize and appreciate
the unique gifts each season has to offer.

May God give you more and more
mercy, peace, and love.

JUDE 2 NLT

The Little Things

Everyday unsung treasures

Chewing Gum

* * * * * *

Lord, I'm so grateful for the little refreshers You have brought into my life. When my spirit needs a quick pick-me-up, I know I can always turn to You. Thank You for refreshing me daily in mind, body, and spirit.

Leaving on Vacation

* * * * * *

Father, thank You for vacations! Thank You for blessing me with this opportunity to relax and gain perspective. Thank You for going with me when I step out of my regular routine. Help me to see You in a new and fresh way while I revel in Your glorious gift of rest.

Tomorrow

* * * * * *

Lord, I am forever glad that no matter what today brings, I can always rely on Your promise of a new day—whether here on earth or with You in heaven. Thank You for this comforting guarantee that sustains my daily hope.

Taking Pictures

• • • • • •

Lord, thank You for this little camera that captures the precious moments of my life. I'm grateful You have provided me a way to vividly remember the special people and places I hold dear. You are a great, wise, and wonderful God.

Every good and perfect gift is from above,
coming down from the Father of
the heavenly lights.

JAMES 1:17 NIV

Parades

• • • • • •

Father, thank You for parades—for smiles, music, and fun. I have much to celebrate—this day and always. Thank You for the joy of celebration.

My Team Wins

* * * * * *

Father, I know that winning isn't everything, but it sure is fun. Thank You for this victory, and help me be a gracious winner.

Singing in Church

* * * * * *

Father, thank You for the chorus of voices around me and for blessing me with a voice to join in. Remind me that You delight in hearing every voice singing Your praises—even those that are a little off-key.

Favorite Song on the Radio

* * * * * *

Father, thank You for this song, for the way it lifts my spirits and brings back so many fond memories. I am so glad You brought music and rejoicing into the world.

Give thanks to the LORD, call on his name;
make known among the nations
what he has done.

PSALM 105:1 NIV

Decorating

* * * * * *

Father, You are a creative God who loves to celebrate. Thank You for sharing Your creativity with me and for the chance to share it with others.

Reflection in the Mirror

* * * * * *

Thank You, Lord, for making me fearfully and wonderfully in Your image. Help me look past the superficial things I may not like about myself to find Your Spirit shining within me.

Janitors

· · · · · ·

Thank You, Father, for the men and women behind the scenes who humbly work so hard to keep things neat and sanitary. The world would be a much less beautiful place without them. Give them strength in their daily tasks, and help me honor them by cleaning up after myself.

First Cookout of the Season

· · · · · ·

Lord, thank You for this simple pleasure: a pleasant evening outdoors and delicious food to share with friends and family. I am so grateful for Your everyday gifts that bring my loved ones together.

Devote yourselves to prayer,
being watchful and thankful.
COLOSSIANS 4:2 NIV

Finding the Perfect Gift

• • • • • •

Father, thank You for blessing me with the
time and resources to find this perfect gift. I am
grateful for the opportunity to show a loved one
how much I care for them. And thank You for the
innumerable perfect gifts You have given me—
especially Your Son, Jesus.

New Baby

• • • • • •

Lord, I am humbled by this miracle of life. I am
filled with hope for the future. Thank You for this
reminder of Your phenomenal love.

Writing a Letter

• • • • • •

Father, I don't sit down to write letters very often,
but thank You for the beauty of the written
word and for giving me the ability to record my
thoughts. Thank You for Your Word and the way
it lifts my spirit. May it be written on my heart
today and always.

Windshield Wipers

· · · · · ·

Father, thank You for windshield wipers and the
warmth inside my car as I drive through this rain.
I don't know what I'd do without a means to see
the path before me clearly. Thank You for always
going before me and keeping all my paths clear—
rain or shine.

*Let every thing that hath breath praise the
LORD. Praise ye the LORD.*
PSALM 150:6 KJV

The Concept of Forever

· · · · · ·

I rejoice in words like *everlasting* and *infinite*,
Father, because Your Word has assured me they
are real. Nothing can ever separate me from
You—not even death. Thank You for the promise
of spending an eternity under Your watchful care.

The Snooze Button

• • • • • •

How I take that extra five minutes for granted, Lord! Thank You for those extra few moments of rest before another hectic day begins. Help me find time throughout the day to rejoice in all Your generous blessings.

Band-Aids

• • • • • •

Thank You for this simple comfort, Father. When I hurt myself, I'm so glad I have a quick remedy to turn to. Though I know a Band-Aid won't heal me, it covers my wound and guards it from infection—just as You cover my sins and heal me from the inside out. I'm so thankful for Your loving care.

Seconds

• • • • • •

Lord, how amazing it is that while I'm planning my life out in months and years, You account for every single second of my day? Help me cherish each and every one now and always.

*A gift is as a precious stone in the eyes
of him that hath it: whithersoever it turneth,
it prospereth.*

PROVERBS 17:8 KJV

Seat Belts

• • • • • •

Father, thank You for the everyday safeguards in
my life that give me a little extra peace of mind
while I'm out and about. I'm forever grateful for
Your care and protection.

Silence

• • • • • •

Thank You, Father, for the gift of peace and
stillness. How often I take it for granted! Help
me discover You in every quiet moment.

Tissues

• • • • • •

Lord, thank You for small comforts when I'm sick or sad. The little things always seem to matter most when I'm in need. When I don't have a tissue handy, thank You for always being there to dry my tears and heal my ills.

White-Out

• • • • • •

Lord, thank You for the ability to cover my mistakes and begin anew. I am grateful for Your promise of forgiveness and the opportunity to be made new again through Your Son, Jesus.

For everything God has created is good,
and nothing is to be thrown away or refused
if it is received with thanksgiving.
1 TIMOTHY 4:4 AMP

Looking at the Stars

* * * * * *

Dear Lord, thank You for the beauty of lights in
the sky. Thank You for the promise that Your Son
will return from heaven with a shout and that
there will be a celebration like no other when He
comes to earth. Thank You for infinite possibilities.

A Good Novel

* * * * * *

Father, thank You for this book to read. Thank
You for the way I can see You whenever I look for
You—even in fiction. I pray that this book will
teach me something about You and the life You
have given me to live.

Good News

* * * * * *

Father, thank You for this good news! Thank You
for every good gift that comes from You. Help me
to stay faithful in the good times and to live my
life with a grateful heart.

Second Chances

• • • • • •

Thank You for the mercy of second chances:
rebounds, the UNDO button on the computer,
and Your generous forgiveness. I am grateful for
the many times You have cleansed my heart and
purified my spirit. Thank You for accepting me,
Lord, imperfections and all.

Because your love is better than life,
my lips will glorify you.

PSALM 63:3 NIV

Surprises

• • • • • •

So many of Your blessings are wonderfully
unexpected, Father. Thank You for finding me
worthy of Your love—and for sending me Your
gifts when You recognize that I am most in need.

Christmas Cards

· · · · · ·

When I think of all the Christmas cards I've received, Father, I realize how truly blessed I am with friends and loved ones who care. Thank You for all the simple pleasures of the holiday season.

Spell-Checker

· · · · · ·

Father, thank You for the fail-safes in my life that gently correct my mistakes. Thank You for Your wise discipline. Help me to focus on my strengths rather than my weaknesses.

Wrinkle-Free Clothing

· · · · · ·

Father, thank You for this blessed time-saver! May I use the time I've saved to praise You for Your daily goodness and everyday miracles.

Then was our mouth filled with laughter,
and our tongue with singing: then said
*they among the heathen, The L*ORD *hath*
done great things for them.

PSALM 126:2 KJV

Socks

• • • • • •

Lord, socks are such a simple blessing that I
barely worry when one goes missing in the
dryer. Thank You for the warmth and protection
they provide. Help me keep all Your gifts in
perspective and never take any of them for
granted—from the ordinary to the extraordinary.

Rest Areas

• • • • • •

Father, thank You for designated areas of rest while I am on the road. I can be in such a hurry sometimes to go as fast and as far as I can. Help me remember that it's important to honor Your gift of rest no matter where I may be.

Day Planners

• • • • • •

Lord, thank You for organization that conquers chaos. As I script out my life from day to day, help me always remember that Your plans come first. May I never be too busy to do Your will.

Headlights

• • • • • •

Father, thank You for bright lights that guide me to my nighttime destinations. It's such a blessing to have my path illuminated in the darkness. May I always walk in Your light as I travel though life on my way to Your kingdom.

Worship the LORD your God, and his blessing will be on your food and water.

EXODUS 23:25 NIV

Security

• • • • • •

Father, thank You for metal detectors, security systems, law enforcement, and all the things that give me peace of mind when I am away from home or all by myself. The world can be a frightening place, but I'm grateful that You are with me always. With You, I truly have nothing to fear.

Long-Distance Phone Calls

• • • • • •

Lord, thank You for the ability to communicate with my faraway friends and family with ease. It's such a blessing to hear their voices by just pushing a few buttons. Help me remember to keep You at the top of my speed-dial list. I'm so very grateful that You're eager to hear from me 24/7.

Hotel Bibles

· · · · · ·

I am so thankful that Your Word is everywhere, Father. Guide readers as they open Your Book, and lead them to the truth of Your unconditional love and amazing promise of salvation.

Lofty Dreams

· · · · · ·

Father, thank You for giving me the ability to dream big and set lofty goals for myself. I know that by Your will, all things are possible. Thank You for including me in Your master plan and helping me see my dreams to fruition.

From the fullness of his grace we have all received one blessing after another.
JOHN 1:16 NIV

Good Advice

* * * * * *

Lord, good advice is truly invaluable, and I'm so thankful for the friends and acquaintances You've brought into my life who have led me down the right paths—even when I wasn't very receptive to their wise counsel. Thank You for always being there to listen to my troubles and for blessing me with caring individuals who tell me what I need to hear—not always what I want to hear.

Coupons

* * * * * *

Lord, every little bit counts, and I'm grateful for all the small ways You help me provide for my family. Thank You for endowing me with wisdom and frugality.

Express Checkout

* * * * * *

Lord, thank You for constant blessings that I can always count on, like the express checkout line. On days when nothing seems to go right, I'm grateful for these time-saving conveniences that are always there for me.

Road Maps

• • • • • •

Father, thank You for detailed maps that show me exactly how to get to where I'm going as I travel from place to place. It's so good to have reliable directions at my fingertips. Thank You for providing me with a moral compass, too, as I navigate to my final destination: You.

The blessing of the LORD brings wealth,

and he adds no trouble to it.

PROVERBS 10:22 NIV

Naps

• • • • • •

Thank You for opportunities, Lord, to refresh and recharge. Help me use the energy I gain to ease the burdens of others who are tired and overworked.

Elastic Waistbands

• • • • • •

Father, thank You for flexibility—not only in the clothing that I wear but also in Your love for me. Even though I am sometimes full of sin, You are always able to wrap Your loving forgiveness snug around me. Thank You for Your one-size-fits-all kind of love.

Home-Cooked Meals

• • • • • •

Thank You for this meal cooked by loving hands, Lord. I am truly blessed by this food and the care that went into making it. Help use this nourishment for Your will.

Happily-Ever-After Endings

• • • • • •

Lord, I know life isn't a fairy tale, but I'm grateful for the hope found in happily-ever-after endings. Help me recognize all the good things You have blessed me with daily and stay focused on the big picture: the ultimate happy ending that You have promised me in heaven.

*Oh that men would praise the LORD
for his goodness, and for his wonderful
works to the children of men!*

PSALM 107:21 KJV

Stopping to Smell the Roses

Refreshing detours from the beaten path

Passing a Cemetery

• • • • • •

Lord, I am so grateful that no one walks the earth or leaves it without Your knowledge. Thank You for the people and stories represented by these stones. Thank You for the ones I hold dear.

Passing a Wedding

• • • • • •

Thank You, Jesus, for the sacrament of marriage and its personal illustration of Your love for the church. Thank You for new beginnings and the joy of celebration.

Garage Sales

• • • • • •

Father, compared to most of the world, we are wealthy beyond belief. We have so much stuff that even our garages are filled with items we no longer want or can use. Help me use my wealth wisely to honor You.

At the Mall

Dear Lord, the people here at the mall represent so many different walks of life. Help me to see them through Your eyes and love them as You do. Thank You for the beauty of diversity and the breadth and depth of Your love for each of us.

The LORD has done great things for us,
and we are filled with joy.

PSALM 126:3 NIV

Voting

Father, thank You for the opportunity to cast my vote. Though I may not always be motivated, I am grateful for the freedoms that come with living in a democracy. Help me make wise decisions concerning our leaders.

Making a Craft

* * * * * *

Lord, thank You for the gift of creativity. Thank You for giving me the time and ability to construct things with my hands. Help me bless someone with my creative endeavors today.

In a Crowd

* * * * * *

Father, I can see how people feel lonely in a crowd. Thank You for the companions You've given me on life's journey. Thank You that even in a crowd, I am uniquely loved by You.

Car Getting Repaired

* * * * * *

Lord, I'd rather not be getting my car repaired, but I am grateful that I will soon be able to travel safely again. Thank You for the mechanic who knows how to fix what's wrong. I pray that You would bless him as he helps service this vehicle on which I rely so much.

Be joyful in hope, patient in affliction,
faithful in prayer.

ROMANS 12:12 NIV

Stuck at a Railroad Crossing

• • • • • •

Heavenly Father, thank You for this time-out in my busy day to sit quietly and reflect. Thank You for the trains that bring us the things we need and take us where we want to go.

At the Library

• • • • • •

Lord, thank You for the silence in this library. Thank You for the bounty of books and endless shelves of reading material. Even though this place is rich with knowledge, help me always be mindful that You are wiser still.

Purchasing the Thanksgiving Turkey

• • • • • •

Lord, there are so many turkeys to choose from. Whether I want one that's big or small, roasted or fried, I can have my choice. We are blessed beyond belief. Thank You for providing food for our nourishment and our pleasure.

A New Business Opens

• • • • • •

Lord, I see a new business has opened in my community. Thank You for the new hope and opportunity there. I pray that You would bless the owners and the employees and guide them in becoming a productive part of the community.

"I will send down showers in season;
there will be showers of blessing."
EZEKIEL 34:26 NIV

Waiting to See the Doctor

• • • • • •

Father, I am amazed at the intricacy and miracle of the human body. Thank You for the privilege of receiving quality medical care. Bless my doctors, and give them wisdom as they care for me.

Waiting for an Ambulance to Pass

• • • • • •

Lord, thank You for medical care that is readily available to us anytime we call. Thank You for the flashing lights and the urgency with which professionals respond to our needs. Protect and bless them on their way.

Waiting for a Restaurant Table

• • • • • •

Lord, I can become so impatient waiting for good things to come. Thank You for this special time away from home and the company of those I'm with. Help me stay positive and focused on the good things You have blessed me with right now.

Passing the Collection Plate

• • • • • •

Lord, thank You for the bountiful blessings You
have bestowed on our church community. Thank
You for the generosity of everyone around me.
Help me to follow their example as I offer my
contribution. May these tithes bring prosperity to
our church and those in need.

*Thus you will be enriched in all things
and in every way, so that you can be
generous, and [your generosity as it is]
administered by us will bring forth
thanksgiving to God.*

2 CORINTHIANS 9:11 AMP

Volunteering

• • • • • •

I am so thankful for this opportunity to donate
my time and energy to a worthy cause, Father.
Thank You for giving me the perfect example
of self-sacrifice in Your Son, Jesus. Guide me in
making my actions speak louder than my words
today.

Washing My Hands

• • • • • •

Lord, thank You for this simple act of hand washing that I take for granted. Thank You for the germ-cleansing power of soap and water and the spirit-cleansing power of Your love.

Pumping Gas

• • • • • •

I always view pumping gas as such a mundane task, Lord, but it's really a small miracle to have such abundant natural resources at my disposal. Thank You for always providing everything I need—I am forever grateful for Your awesome provisions.

Trying on Clothes

• • • • • •

Father, thank You for so many options in dressing up my exterior appearance. Thank You for modest choices that flatter the figure You have blessed me with. Remind me continually that what's on the inside will always matter more to You than what's on the outside.

Praise be to the God and Father of our
Lord Jesus Christ, who has blessed us
in the heavenly realms with every
spiritual blessing in Christ.

EPHESIANS 1:3 NIV

At the Family Reunion

• • • • • •

Lord, help me rejoice in this time with my family today. Thank You for all the ups and downs we've shared together and our rich legacy of hope and trust in You. Thank You for sharing in this celebration with us today.

Another Birthday

• • • • • •

Lord, I don't always look forward to growing another year older, but I thank You for the opportunity to enjoy another year of Your bountiful blessings on earth. Thank You for parties and cake and thoughtful gifts. May I continue to live out my days as a witness to Your goodness.

During a Blackout

* * * * * *

Lord, thank You for the beauty of burning candles illuminating the darkness. Thank You for this time to rediscover how many of Your blessings we take for granted. Thank You for always looking out for us. Help us appreciate this quiet time as a way to strengthen our relationships with those around us.

Ordinary Days

* * * * * *

Father, help me treasure this uneventful day and realize how priceless it truly is. Thank You for another opportunity to learn, grow, live, explore, and love. Help me relish every moment as though it were my last.

Breaking in a New Pair of Shoes

* * * * * *

Lord, it's not always pleasant breaking in a new pair of shoes, but I'm grateful nonetheless for yet another provision. Guide me in these and all my steps down a path of service and goodwill that will glorify You.

*Have the roots [of your being] firmly and
deeply planted [in Him, fixed and founded
in Him], being continually built up in Him,
becoming increasingly more confirmed and
established in the faith, just as you were
taught, and abounding and overflowing
in it with thanksgiving.*

COLOSSIANS 2:7 AMP

Meeting Someone New

Lord, thank You for allowing my path to cross
with this new friend. Help me plant seeds of
kindness in my new friend's life that will inspire
her to know You better.

Coincidences

Lord, thank You for happy coincidences and days
when things seem to just fall into place. Help me
always remember and recognize these moments
as examples of Your awesome power working in
my life. All credit goes to You for the good things
that come my way.

Pulling Weeds

• • • • • •

Father, thank You for the gift of gardening—for the beautiful diversity of plants and flowers in the world. I get so frustrated with the weeds that invade my manicured space, but I know I should be grateful for new life in all forms—no matter how unwelcome they may be. Help me to live in harmony with all Your creation and recognize that You are the ultimate designer of landscapes.

"Giving thanks is a sacrifice that truly honors me."

PSALM 50:23 NLT

Cleaning Up after a Party

• • • • • •

Lord, cleaning up isn't my favorite task, but I know it's a necessary one—especially when You've blessed me abundantly with good friends. Thank You for surrounding me with so many wonderful people. I am grateful for the daily richness they bring to my life.

Someone Honks at Me

· · · · · ·

Lord, thank You for small reminders that I am
not perfect. Help me be a polite and courteous
driver, and guide me in recognizing other areas of
my life where I could improve.

Windy Day

· · · · · ·

Heavenly Father, although I cannot see it, I feel
the wind. You are a holy and awesome God—
even the winds and waves obey You. Thank You
for this tangible example of Your power.

Received a Favor

· · · · · ·

Thank You for this gift, Lord. I feel so
undeserving, yet You saw my need and sent
someone to respond. Thank You for seeing that all
my needs are met.

*When I look at your heavens, the work of your
fingers, the moon and the stars, which you have
set in place, what is man that you are mindful
of him, and the son of man that you care for
him? Yet you have made him a little lower
than the heavenly beings and crowned him
with glory and honor.*

PSALM 8:3–5 ESV

Can't Sleep

• • • • • •

Father, even when I lie awake in the night, You
are with me. Thank You for the rare silence and
the opportunity to speak with You. Thank You for
whispering to my heart—help my ears to hear You.

Anticipation

• • • • • •

Thank You for giving me this thing to look
forward to, Father. I'm so excited that I can hardly
wait! Help me recognize the little joys in each
moment of my life so I will look forward to living
each and every second of the day with hope and
enthusiasm.

Crossing the Street

• • • • • •

Lord, thank You for the safety of crosswalks, for laws, and for giving me a place to go. Help me dedicate all the small moments of my life to You.

Reading the Newspaper

• • • • • •

Lord, there is so much bad news in the world, but I am grateful that You make all things work for good. Thank You for freedom of speech, political diversity, and the refreshing humor of the comics. I pray Your master plan reigns supreme in my life.

"I will make you into a great nation and I will bless you; I will make your name great, and you will be a blessing. I will bless those who bless you, and whoever curses you I will curse; and all peoples on earth will be blessed through you."

GENESIS 12:2–3 NIV

A Light Load

• • • • • •

Father, You have given me such a good life. I've had my ups and downs, but all Your burdens are blessings in disguise. Thank You for giving me a light load to carry on my journey to You.

An Airplane Flies Overhead

• • • • • •

Lord, thank You for endowing man with the inspiration and wisdom to soar like a bird. You have blessed us with such staggering brainpower. Help us use it for good and in ways that will benefit all Your creation.

Passing a Farm

• • • • • •

You have blessed us with such abundant (and delicious!) resources, Lord. Thank You for bountiful harvests and for friends and loved ones gathered around my table.

Wrapping Gifts

Father, thank You for these gifts to wrap. Thank You
for my loved ones, who are the true gift. Help me to
be a blessing to them as they have blessed me.

*The LORD gave, and the LORD hath taken
away; blessed be the name of the LORD.*

JOB 1:21 KJV

Finding the
Silver Lining

Recognizing the good in everything

When My Faith Is Challenged

• • • • • •

Father, thank You for the truth of Your Word
and for always providing me with a ready answer
when I am questioned by those who haven't
yet experienced the saving grace of Your Son.
Thank You for this opportunity to be a light to
the world—to share Your glorious promises with
others and bring them closer to an understanding
of Your unconditional love.

When My Heart Is Broken

• • • • • •

Lord, You are the healer of all things broken
and despairing. Thank You for this opportunity
to put things into perspective and grow in my
relationship with You. I don't have much to offer,
but I know that in Your loving embrace my
tattered spirit will become new again.

A Full Medicine Cabinet

• • • • •

Father, there are so many pills and bottles in my
medicine cabinet that opening the door causes
a veritable avalanche. But instead of focusing on
the ills these medications treat, help me celebrate
their healing qualities. Thank You for all the
miracles of modern medicine, big and small.

Receiving a Disappointing Gift

· · · · · ·

Lord, help me be thankful for every gift that comes my way—even if it's not what I wanted or was expecting. Big or small, expensive or thrifty, it is truly a blessing to receive gifts of any kind. Thank You for this thoughtful gesture, and help me celebrate with genuine gratitude.

You have turned for me my mourning into dancing; You have loosed my sackcloth and girded me with gladness.
PSALM 30:11 NASB

Speeding Tickets

· · · · · ·

Thank You for this reminder to slow down, Lord. Getting a speeding ticket is a hard way to learn, and I'm not eager to accept the consequences of my actions—but with Your help, I know I can become a more conscientious driver and individual.

Stale Bread

• • • • • •

Father, thank You for blessing my family with so much food that we can't consume it quickly enough! Guide us in wasting fewer of Your precious resources, and help us use Your daily bread for Your will.

Gray Hair and Laugh Lines

• • • • • •

Aging isn't easy, Father, but I'm glad You have blessed me with a full life. Help me recognize these gray hairs and wrinkles as testaments to Your gifts of wisdom, laughter, and grace.

My Team Loses

• • • • • •

Lord, losing isn't fun. It's hard to put forth so much effort and to end in defeat, but help me see this loss in the light of eternity. Thank You that this loss is temporary and for the promise that You've won the only victory that matters.

Our hearts ache, but we always have joy.

We are poor, but we give spiritual riches to others.

We own nothing, and yet we have everything.

2 CORINTHIANS 6:10 NLT

Losing Something of Sentimental Value

Father, losing something precious has taught me that things are just things—that what is most important in life is cherishing my relationship with You above all else. I may have lost part of a special memory today, but I know I can never lose You. Thank You for being with me forever and always.

The Check-Engine Light

Dear Father, thank You for the check-engine light that warns me of trouble. Though I may not acknowledge its appearance joyfully, I'm thankful that I can count on it to identify problems before any damage is done. Help me recognize the value of Your warnings and praise You for the consistency of Your love and care.

The Anniversary of a Loss

• • • • • •

Father, today is a sad day, and I am reminded of my loss. Thank You for the peace You bring to my soul and for the promise that weeping only lasts for the night and joy comes in the morning.

Eating Alone

• • • • • •

Lord, it's hard to be left out, but thank You that I am not truly alone. Thank You for Your presence and for the people I do have in my life. Thank You for caring for me when I feel that no one else does.

When you have eaten and are satisfied,
praise the LORD your God for the good
land he has given you.

DEUTERONOMY 8:10 NIV

Driving an Old Car

• • • • • •

Though I may dream about driving a shiny new car, Lord, I'm grateful for this one that has served me so reliably over the years. Give me a grateful heart, Father, and help me avoid coveting unnecessary luxuries.

Unused Sick Days

• • • • • •

Lord, thank You for keeping me well this year. I wish I could take advantage of more time off, but I know I need to be in the workplace, shining the light of Your Son's example into the lives of all those I encounter. Help me do productive work in Your name every day I am able.

Unanswered Prayers

• • • • • •

It amazes me, Father, how You know my needs so intimately. Thank You for listening to all my prayers—even the unreasonable ones—and providing me with comfort and direction. Your ways are mysterious, but I'm grateful that You always have the big picture in mind.

Sunburn

· · · · · ·

Father, thank You for sunshine and warm, cloudless days. Sometimes I get so excited about rejoicing in the weather outdoors that I forget to protect my skin properly. Help me heal quickly so I can start enjoying the delicious warmth of summertime again soon.

In the day of prosperity be joyful, but in the day of adversity consider: Surely God has appointed the one as well as the other, so that man can find out nothing that will come after him.

ECCLESIASTES 7:14 NKJV

When I Forget an Umbrella

· · · · · ·

Lord, give me a child's heart today, and help me rejoice in this rain. So what if I get a little wet? Thank You for puddles to jump in and rainbows after the storm.

Discipline

* * * * * *

Thank You, Father, for Your firm and consistent correction. I do not like to be disciplined, but I know it's for my own good. Open my mind, and help me face the consequences of my actions with dignity and humility.

When the Unexpected Happens

* * * * * *

Lord, thank You for unpredictability in life. Though it's hard sometimes, I'm glad that only You know what the future holds. Thank You for allowing me to live one moment at a time.

When My Plans Fall Through

* * * * * *

Lord, let this disappointment be a reminder that nothing in life is set in stone—except You. Thank You for being there to uplift and comfort me when all else is lost.

Everything God created is good, and nothing is to be rejected if it is received with thanksgiving.

1 TIMOTHY 4:4 NIV

When I'm under Pressure

Lord, thank You for all those who rely on me at home, at work, and in my daily life. It is a good feeling to be needed. Give me strength to fulfill my duties and obligations to the best of my ability. I leave the rest in Your capable hands, Father.

Embarrassment

Lord, thank You for this humbling moment. I need reminders sometimes that I am only human. Thank You for loving and forgiving me in spite of myself.

Uncertainty

· · · · · ·

I confess, Lord, that I do not like uncertainty. It is tempting to become anxious because I don't know how this is going to turn out. Thank You for being here with me and for holding my future so gently and carefully in Your loving hands. I know You will help me become a stronger person no matter the outcome.

Temptation

· · · · · ·

Father, thank You for gracing me with the gift of free will. I am so grateful for Your trust in my ability to make my own decisions. Thank You for consequences that remind me of what's right and what's wrong. Give me a heart that strives for right. Though temptation can be hard to resist, I know it is fleeting. Only Your goodness will last an eternity.

"So do not fear, for I am with you; do not be dismayed, for I am your God. I will strengthen you and help you; I will uphold you with my righteous right hand."

ISAIAH 41:10 NIV

When I've Been Offended

• • • • • •

Jesus, my heart hurts, but I thank You for this pain because it means I am alive and real. I know that I will grow through this adversity. Help me to forgive as You have forgiven me.

Bad News

• • • • • •

Lord, I know this news was not a surprise to You, but it has caught me off guard. Thank You for the promise that You can bring good out of every situation—even the ones that seem very bad to me. Help me trust You to see me through.

The GPS Fails

• • • • • •

When I'm lost, Father, my initial reaction is to feel frustrated and scared. Help me recognize the times I'm lost as opportunities to explore and discover new people, places, and things—new blessings. And when I stray too far off the beaten path, thank You for being the Good Shepherd who guides me back to where I belong.

Extreme Weather

• • • • • •

Father, thank You for the awesome power of Your creation. Though I may tremble in the face of storms, remind me that no storm lasts forever and that You are always cradling me securely in the palm of Your hand.

The LORD is my strength and my shield;
my heart trusts in him, and I am helped.

PSALM 28:7 NIV

Daylight Savings Time

• • • • • •

Father, I dread losing an hour of precious sleep, but I know, like everything else, this, too, shall pass. Thank You for the blessing of sunshine and for giving us the wisdom to recognize our need for conservation. Thank You for all the little ways we are able to honor Your creation.

Losing a Job

* * * * * *

Lord, thank You for this opportunity to explore
the many spiritual and physical gifts You have
bestowed on me. Help me overcome my feelings
of abandonment and betrayal and open my
mind to discover the rich possibilities that are all
around me. Thank You for being my wellspring of
hope in times of need.

Scars

* * * * * *

Lord, thank You for these reminders of the trials
and hurts I have overcome. I am so grateful for
the blessings of strength, healing, and hope You've
brought into my life.

Hard Work

* * * * * *

Father, I am happy for this productive work
You have given me to do. Thank You for the
satisfaction that comes from a job well done and
for giving me a strong, disciplined spirit.

*It is God's gift that all should eat and
drink and take pleasure in all their toil.*

ECCLESIASTES 3:13 NRSV

101
THANKSGIVING
Blessings

INTRODUCTION

What are you thankful for this Thanksgiving? Food, family, friendship, shelter, love—all of these are important blessings for which to give thanks. But our gratitude can encompass so much more. From sharing coffee with a friend to a rainbow after a storm and good health to beautiful artwork, use the 101 blessings in this book as a way to widen and deepen your thankfulness to the Giver of all good things. Then and only then will you experience true Thanksgiving.

1.
THE LOVE OF FAMILY.

And I will bless them that bless thee, and curse him that curseth thee:
and in thee shall all families of the earth be blessed.
GENESIS 12:3

2.
TRUE FRIENDS WHO
ARE THERE REGARDLESS
OF CIRCUMSTANCES.

A friend loveth at all times.
PROVERBS 17:17

3.
GOD'S WORD,
THE BREAD OF LIFE.

*It is written, That man shall not live by bread alone,
but by every word of God.*
LUKE 4:4

4.
FREEDOM OF WORSHIP.

I will worship toward thy holy temple, and praise thy name.
PSALM 138:2

5.
BEAUTIFUL MUSIC TO ENJOY.

Sing unto him a new song;
play skilfully with a loud noise.
PSALM 33:3

6.
THE WARMTH OF A FIRE IN WINTER.

I will praise thee, O LORD, with my whole heart;
I will shew forth all thy marvellous works.
PSALM 9:1

7.
OUR FOREFATHERS WHO PAVED THE WAY FOR US.

*Thus saith the L*ORD*, Stand ye in the ways, and see, and ask for the old paths, where is the good way, and walk therein.*
JEREMIAH 6:16

8.
A MOTHER'S LOVE.

For I was my father's son,
tender and only beloved in the sight of my other.

PROVERBS 4:3

9.
THE SINGING OF BIRDS.

The flowers appear on the earth; the time of the singing of birds is come,
and the voice of the turtle dove is heard in our land.
SONG OF SOLOMON 2:12

10.
RAIN IN DUE SEASON.

Then I will give you rain in due season, and the land shall yield her
increase, and the trees of the field shall yield their fruit.
LEVITICUS 26:4

11.
TWO HANDS TO
PERFORM TASKS.

Whatsoever thy hand findeth to do, do it with thy might;
for there is no work, nor device, nor knowledge, nor wisdom,
in the grave, whither thou goest.
ECCLESIASTES 9:10

12.
LAUGHTER TO
EXPRESS OUR JOY.

Then was our mouth filled with laughter,
and our tongue with singing: then said they among the heathen,
The LORD hath done great things for them.
PSALM 126:2

13.
THE ACT OF FORGIVENESS.

*And be ye kind one to another, tenderhearted, forgiving one another,
even as God for Christ's sake hath forgiven you.*
EPHESIANS 4:32

14.
SPRING FLOWERS.

*Thou waterest the ridges thereof abundantly: thou settlest the
furrows thereof: thou makest it soft
with showers: thou blessest the springing thereof.*
PSALM 65:10

15.
AUTUMN LEAF COLOR.

To every thing there is a season,
and a time to every purpose under the heaven.
ECCLESIASTES 3:1

16.
THE INSTRUCTION
OF A FATHER.

My son, hear the instruction of thy father, and forsake not the law of
thy mother: for they shall be an ornament of grace unto thy head.
PROVERBS 1:8–9

17.
THE INNOCENCE OF CHILDREN.

But Jesus said, Suffer little children, and forbid them not, to come unto me: for of such is the kingdom of heaven.
MATTHEW 19:14

18.
PEACEFUL SLEEP.

I will both lay me down in peace, and sleep: for thou, LORD, only makest me dwell in safety.
PSALM 4:8

19.
TEARS EXPRESSING OUR JOY OR GRIEF.

They that sow in tears shall reap in joy.
PSALM 126:5

20.
A SISTER'S LOVE.

Charity suffereth long, and is kind; charity envieth not;
charity vaunteth not itself, is not puffed up.
1 CORINTHIANS 13:4

21.
SUNSHINE AFTER STORMS.

The day is thine, the night also is thine:
thou hast prepared the light and the sun.
PSALM 74:16

22.
THE ABILITY TO LEARN.

A wise man will hear, and will increase learning; and a man of
understanding shall attain unto wise counsels.
PROVERBS 1:5

23.
KIND WORDS.

A man hath joy by the answer of his mouth:
and a word spoken in due season, how good is it!
PROVERBS 15:23

24.
THE PURSUIT OF
HAPPINESS.

Happy is he that hath the God of Jacob for his help,
whose hope is in the LORD his God.
PSALM 146:5

25.
LIPS THAT WORSHIP GOD.

My soul shall be satisfied as with marrow and fatness;
and my mouth shall praise thee with joyful lips.
PSALM 63:5

26.
EYES TO ENJOY THE
WORLD AROUND US.

Truly the light is sweet, and a pleasant thing
it is for the eyes to behold the sun.
ECCLESIASTES 11:7

27.
THE WISDOM OF OUR ELDERS.

Likewise, ye younger, submit yourselves unto the elder.
Yea, all of you be subject one to another.
1 PETER 5:5

28.
FOOD ON OUR TABLE.

And having food and raiment let us be therewith content.
1 TIMOTHY 6:8

29.
GOD-GIVEN TALENTS.

*But now hath God set the members every one of them in the body,
as it hath pleased him.*
1 CORINTHIANS 12:18

30.
A PLACE TO WORSHIP GOD.

*I was glad when they said unto me,
Let us go into the house of the LORD.*
PSALM 122:1

31.
THE WARMTH OF SUNSHINE.

*From the rising of the sun unto the going down
of the same the LORD's name is to be praised.*
PSALM 113:3

32.
FRESH WATER TO DRINK.

*And ye shall serve the LORD your God,
and he shall bless thy bread, and thy water.*
EXODUS 23:25

33.
COOL BREEZES ON A HOT DAY.

*He causeth his wind to blow,
and the waters flow.*
PSALM 147:18

34.
LAUGHTER IN THE MIDST OF SORROW.

*Even in laughter the heart
is sorrowful.*
PROVERBS 14:13

35.
COMFORT FROM A GOOD FRIEND.

Iron sharpeneth iron; so a man sharpeneth
the countenance of his friend.
PROVERBS 27:17

36.
GOD'S PROMISES.

The Lord is not slack concerning his promise, as some men count
slackness; but is longsuffering to us-ward.
2 PETER 3:9

37.
THE DIVERSITY OF THE FOUR SEASONS.

Thou hast set all the borders of the earth:
thou hast made summer and winter.
PSALM 74:17

38.
A VOICE TO SING SONGS.

I will be glad and rejoice in thee:
I will sing praise to thy name, O thou most High.
PSALM 9:2

39.
THE BREATH OF LIFE.

And the Lord God formed man of the dust of the ground,
and breathed into his nostrils the breath of life;
and man became a living soul.
GENESIS 2:7

40.
THE LOVE OF A MATE.

Therefore shall a man leave his father and his mother,
and shall cleave unto his wife: and they shall be one flesh.
GENESIS 2:24

41.
CHILDREN IN THE FAMILY.

Lo, children are an heritage of the LORD:
and the fruit of the womb is his reward.
PSALM 127:3

42.
GOOD HEALTH.

Beloved, I wish above all things that thou mayest prosper
and be in health, even as thy soul prospereth.
3 JOHN 2

43.
A GODLY HERITAGE.

When I call to remembrance the unfeigned faith that is in thee,
which dwelt first in thy grandmother Lois, and thy
mother Eunice; and I am persuaded that in thee also.
2 TIMOTHY 1:5

44.
EARS TO HEAR.

The ear that heareth the reproof of life abideth among the wise.
PROVERBS 15:31

45.
COFFEE WITH A FRIEND.

He that is of a merry heart hath a continual feast.
PROVERBS 15:15

46.
THE CONFIDENCE
OF A FRIEND.

A talebearer revealeth secrets:
but he that is of a faithful spirit concealeth the matter.
PROVERBS 11:13

47.
TIME SPENT WITH FAMILY.

Blessed is every one that feareth the LORD; that walketh in his ways.
Thy wife shall be as a fruitful vine by the sides of thine house:
thy children like olive plants round about thy table.
PSALM 128:1, 3

48.
A GODLY MENTOR.

Where no counsel is, the people fall:
but in the multitude of counsellors there is safety.
PROVERBS 11:14

49.
PRODUCTIVE GARDENS.

Build ye houses, and dwell in them;
and plant gardens, and eat the fruit of them.
JEREMIAH 29:5

50.
TIME SPENT CONVERSING WITH GOD.

I love them that love me;
and those that seek me early shall find me.
PROVERBS 8:17

51.
LETTERS FROM A LOVED ONE.

Heaviness in the heart of man maketh it stoop:
but a good word maketh it glad.
PROVERBS 12:25

52.
A REPORT OF GOOD NEWS.

As cold waters to a thirsty soul,
so is good news from a far country.
PROVERBS 25:25

53.
INSPIRING, CARING TEACHERS.

Give instruction to a wise man, and he will be yet wiser:
teach a just man, and he will increase in learning.
PROVERBS 9:9

54.
THE DESIRE FOR AN ABUNDANT LIFE.

I am come that they might have life,
and that they might have it more abundantly.
JOHN 10:10

55.
HOPE FOR TOMORROW.

For thou art my hope, O Lord GOD:
thou art my trust from my youth.
PSALM 71:5

56.
GOOD BOOKS TO READ.

Whoso loveth instruction loveth knowledge.
PROVERBS 12:1

57.
THE GIFT OF GOD'S GRACE.

For by grace are ye saved through faith;
and that not of yourselves: it is the gift of God.
EPHESIANS 2:8

58.
COURAGE TO PURSUE OUR DREAMS.

I can do all things through Christ which strengtheneth me.
PHILIPPIANS 4:13

59.
THE COMFORT OF
A BED FOR SLEEPING.

Stand in awe, and sin not:
commune with your own heart upon your bed, and be still.
PSALM 4:4

60.
THE BEAUTY OF THE STARS
ON A DARK NIGHT.

When I consider thy heavens, the work of thy fingers,
the moon and the stars, which thou hast ordained;
what is man, that thou art mindful of him?
PSALM 8:3–4

61.
THE COMPANIONSHIP OF ANIMALS.

*And out of the ground the LORD God formed every beast of the field,
and every fowl of the air; and brought them unto Adam to see what he
would call them: and whatsoever Adam called every living creature,
that was the name thereof.*
GENESIS 2:19

62.
THE HARVEST OF
A GARDEN.

*For thou shalt eat the labour of thine hands:
happy shalt thou be, and it shall be well with thee.*
PSALM 128:2

63.
MODERN TECHNOLOGY.

When the wise is instructed,
he receiveth knowledge.
PROVERBS 21:11

64.
REST AFTER HARD WORK.

Six days thou shalt do thy work,
and on the seventh day thou shalt rest.
EXODUS 23:12

65.
PRAYER OFFERED FOR
YOU BY A FRIEND.

*Confess your faults one to another, and pray one for another,
that ye may be healed. The effectual fervent prayer of a
righteous man availeth much.*
JAMES 5:16

66.
BEAUTIFUL ARTWORK.

I will call upon the LORD, who is worthy to be praised.
PSALM 18:3

67.
THE SKILL OF A GOOD DOCTOR.

Many are the afflictions of the righteous:
but the LORD delivereth him out of them all.
PSALM 34:19

68.
RAINBOWS AFTER
A STORM.

And it shall come to pass, when I bring a cloud over the earth,
that the bow shall be seen in the cloud.
GENESIS 9:14

69.
FRIENDS WITH STRONG SHOULDERS TO LEAN ON.

Ointment and perfume rejoice the heart:
so doth the sweetness of a man's friend by hearty counsel.
PROVERBS 27:9

70.
FAMILY HOLIDAY CELEBRATIONS.

Behold, how good and how pleasant it is for
brethren to dwell together in unity!
PSALM 133:1

71.
Air-conditioning in the summer.

O give thanks unto the Lord; call upon his name:
make known his deeds among the people.
PSALM 105:1

72.
Mentors who care.

The rich and poor meet together:
the Lord is the maker of them all.
PROVERBS 22:2

73.
AN UNEXPECTED VALENTINE.

Beloved, let us love one another: for love is of God;
and every one that loveth is born of God, and knoweth God.
1 JOHN 4:7

74.
GOD'S MERCY.

For the LORD is good; his mercy is everlasting;
and his truth endureth to all generations.
PSALM 100:5

75.
INNER JOY THAT
MAKES YOU SMILE.

Thou wilt shew me the path of life: in thy presence is fulness of joy;
at thy right hand there are pleasures for evermore.
PSALM 16:11

76.
EMPLOYMENT.

Whatsoever thy hand findeth to do, do it with thy might.
ECCLESIASTES 9:10

77.
THE ABILITY TO LAUGH.

A merry heart doeth good like a medicine.
PROVERBS 17:22

78.
THE SHADE OF
A BIG TREE.

The shady trees cover him with their shadow;
the willows of the brook compass him about.
JOB 40:22

79.
VICTORY AFTER A BATTLE.

For whatsoever is born of God overcometh the world:
and this is the victory that overcometh the world, even our faith.
1 JOHN 5:4

80.
STRENGTH TO RUN
A RACE.

For by thee I have run through a troop;
and by my God have I leaped over a wall.
PSALM 18:29

81.
THE SMALL THINGS IN LIFE.

Bless the LORD, O my soul, and forget not all his benefits.
PSALM 103:2

82.
SPIRITUAL DIRECTION.

Blessed is the man that walketh not in the counsel
of the ungodly, nor standeth in the way of sinners,
nor sitteth in the seat of the scornful.
PSALM 1:1

83.
A FIELD OF WILDFLOWERS.

The glory of the LORD shall endure for ever:
the LORD shall rejoice in his works.
PSALM 104:31

84.
THE MAJESTY OF MOUNTAINS.

As the mountains are round about Jerusalem, so the LORD is round
about his people from henceforth even for ever.
PSALM 125:2

85.
THE DESIRE TO SMILE.

Happy is that people, whose God is the LORD.
PSALM 144:15

86.
TIME TO SMELL THE ROSES.

Be still, and know that I am God.
PSALM 46:10

87.
OPPORTUNITIES TO IMPROVE YOURSELF.

Hear, ye children, the instruction of a father,
and attend to know understanding.
PROVERBS 4:1

88.
COMMUNICATION WITH OTHERS.

Righteous lips are the delight of kings;
and they love him that speaketh right.

PROVERBS 16:13

89.
COMMON COURTESY FROM OTHERS.

Look not every man on his own things,
but every man also on the things of others.
PHILIPPIANS 2:4

90.
LEISURE TIME WITH FRIENDS.

Be kindly affectioned one to another with brotherly love;
in honour preferring one another.
ROMANS 12:10

91.
THE ABILITY TO PROVIDE FOR YOUR FAMILY.

She looketh well to the ways of her household,
and eateth not the bread of idleness.
PROVERBS 31:27

92.
WORDS OF WISDOM FROM A FRIEND.

Hear counsel, and receive
instruction, that thou mayest
be wise in thy latter end.
PROVERBS 19:20

93.
A NEW DAY.

This is the day which the LORD hath made;
we will rejoice and be glad in it.
PSALM 118:24

94.
BEAUTIFUL POETRY.

The Lord gave the word:
great was the company of
those that published it.
PSALM 68:11

95.
COURAGE WHEN NEEDED.

Be strong and of a good courage, fear not, nor be afraid of them:
*for the L*ORD *thy God, he it is that doth go with thee;*
he will not fail thee, nor forsake thee.
DEUTERONOMY 31:6

96.
CONTENTMENT.

But godliness with contentment is great gain.
1 TIMOTHY 6:6

97.
A BEAUTIFUL SUNSET.

He appointed the moon for seasons:
the sun knoweth his going down.
PSALM 104:19

98.
A PHONE CALL FROM AN
OLD FRIEND OR RELATIVE.

Pleasant words are as an honeycomb, sweet to the soul,
and health to the bones.
PROVERBS 16:24

99.
EARLY MORNING SOLITUDE WITH GOD.

My meditation of him shall be sweet:
I will be glad in the LORD.
PSALM 104:34

100.
THE POWER AND BEAUTY OF A RIVER.

He sendeth the springs into the valleys,
which run among the hills.
PSALM 104:10

101.
THE PRIVILEGE OF DOING GOOD FOR OTHERS.

*Withhold not good from them to whom it is due,
when it is in the power of thine hand to do it.*

PROVERBS 3:27